Floragami
Armin Täubner

D0477997

STACKPOLE BOOKS

0 11557 01336 8

▶09

▶29

▶79

CONTENTS

48

Introduction

Floragami is a perfect technique for anyone who loves folding paper. The foundation of this process are the folds like the ones used in origami. Due to the wide variety of techniques and paper types you can use, floragami offers numerous design and application possibilities. In this book, you will find a collection of the most beautiful floragami ideas. From delicate single flowers to extraordinary flower decorations, there is something here for everyone! We hope you have fun!

SINGLE FLOWERS

As an eternally fresh bouquet in a vase or an elegant table decoration, folded paper flowers are always eye-catchers. Wonderful decorations and unique gift ideas, these delicate blossoms spread joy and the feeling of spring. Let yourself be inspired and create beautiful works of floragami that never wither.

Elegant Lilies
simple and classy

FLOWER DIAMETER
approximately 5 in.

MATERIALS
FOR EACH FLOWER

- Sheet of white paper, 20 lbs., 6 in. square
- Sheet of transparent yellow silkworm paper, 10 lbs., 4 in. square
- 12 in. aluminum wire in white, no more than 2 mm in diameter
- Adhesive putty

FOLDING INSTRUCTIONS
Lily Flowers: Flowers A and B

Page 103–104

1 Fold a Flower A from the white paper, following the instructions on pages 103–104. At the base of the flower, cut off the tip. This is where the aluminum wire will be inserted and glued for the stem (see image 1).

2 Fold a Flower B (see page 103) out of the smaller yellow paper. Press the flowers, opening up the sections so that, when seen from above, they have a cross shape. Glue the yellow flowers inside the white lilies.

3 Make a small ball (no more than ½ in.) out of the adhesive putty; daub it with glue and place it on the end of the wire. Insert the other end of the wire through the flower from above until the putty ball is located at the tip of the flower. Pinch the tip of the flower to affix it to the adhesive putty and let the glue dry.

1

2   **3**

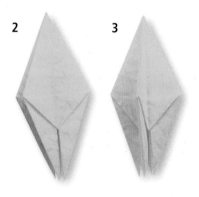

Tip

These lilies look great when there are several hung together (around a candleholder, for example). They are also great to use as gift tags.

Dreams of Flowers in Blue

for versatile decorating

FLOWER DIAMETER
approximately 4 in.

MATERIALS
- 8 sheets of two-sided paper (light and dark blue), 18 lbs., 16 in. square

FOLDING INSTRUCTIONS
Stamen Flowers: Flowers with a Ring of Stamens
Pages 99–101

Cut the paper into quarters so that the flowers are not too large (4 in. square). Fold eight petals for each flower, following the directions on pages 99–101.

1 Press together each finished, glued petal, and crease the side to give the petal a point.

2 Apply the glue to the area colored in red, below.

3+4 Glue the petals together.

Flowers in Pastel Shades

a creative use for paper baking cups

FLOWER DIAMETER

approximately 5 in.

MATERIALS
(PER FLOWER)

- 12 small paper baking cups in pink, light blue, yellow, or purple, no larger than 2 in. in diameter (at the bottom)

FOLDING INSTRUCTIONS

Rose Flowers: Flower A, Variation 1, and Flower B, Variation 1

Pages 116–118

Tip: Please see the instructions for working with paper baking cups on page 116.

1 Fold six paper baking cups (for best results, use ones with a white inner surface) according to the instructions for Flower A, Variation 1 (pages 116–117), starting with the white side facing upwards.

2 Fold the other six paper baking cups according to the instructions for Flower B, Variation 1 (pages 117–118), with the pink side up, to get flowers with pink inner surfaces.

3 Glue the flowers with the pink inner surfaces (flower B) together into a star. Glue the flowers with white on the inside in the spaces between the pink ones.

4 The second flower pictured at left was made with the same process, with light blue and white paper baking cups. The third flower was made with yellow/white and purple/white paper baking cups.

Charming Flowers
in spring colors

FLOWER DIAMETER
approximately 6 in.

MATERIALS
FOR EACH FLOWER

- 10 doilies in light blue, light green, or pink, 6½ in. in diameter
- Wooden dowel, ¼ in. in diameter, 20 in. long
- Acrylic paint in white
- Small sponge

FOLDING INSTRUCTIONS
Rose Flowers: Flower A, Variation 2
Pages 116–117

Tip: **Please see the instructions on how to work with doilies on page 116.**

1 Fold all ten doilies up to the eighth folding step of the instructions for Flower A, Variation 2 (pages 116–117). Then apply glue to and fold in the two side corners, as shown in step 9 on page 117.

2 Then, right away, raise both the light blue portions of each edge so that they do not stick to the medium blue background. Otherwise, the glue will penetrate through the lace border, sticking everything together and preventing the petals from spreading open later. Let all ten pieces dry for an hour.

3 Follow step 9 from page 117 for all ten parts and let dry again.

4 After an hour, the dry flower petals can be glued together to form a flower. It is recommended that you not glue all of the flower petals together at once but rather make two groups of three and a group of four and then wait a bit before gluing them together. Let the glue dry.

5 Sharpen the dowels just a little, with either a knife or a pencil sharpener. Use the sponge to paint the dowels.

6 Attach each flower to the pointed end of a dowel.

Tip

You can also make these flowers using round oragami paper. This paper is much easier to glue; small amounts of glue dry immediately on the thin paper, and you can move on quickly.

Bright and Colorful Summer Flowers

a great gift to bring to a summer party

FLOWER DIAMETER
approximately 7½ in.

MATERIALS
- 6 sheets of polka-dot paper, orange and yellow or purple and lilac, 6 in. square
- Green construction paper
- 12 in. green-paper–covered wire, 2 mm in diameter
- Pliers
- Wire cutters

FOLDING INSTRUCTIONS
Garden Flowers: Simple Flowers (with variation on this page)
Page 121

TEMPLATE
Page 125

1 Fold three flower petals using polka-dot paper according to the drawings on page 121, steps 1–16. Take the other three sheets and then fold three flower petals for steps 1–14, then continue with steps 15a to 18a, below. Glue the two petal types together to create a flower.

2 Create a flower stalk by bending the wire in half and twisting the two halves together. Cut off a 1-inch piece of one of the two wires. Insert the longer wire into the center of the flower before you glue the first petal to the last one.

3 Trace the leaf pattern (see page 28). Transfer the outline two or three times to the construction paper and cut it out. Fold each leaf (on the dotted line) and glue it to the wire.

Variation

15a+16a In this variation, the triangular tips are coated with glue (yellow lines) and folded down on the red lines.

17a Apply glue to the right folded section (yellow line) and then fold the left half to the right.

18a Combine these petals into a single flower by applying glue to the area marked in yellow.

Work slowly and precisely as you fold and assemble the flowers. Only then will they be perfect.

Flower Arrangements for the Table

an eye-catching decoration for any occasion

FLOWER DIAMETER
approximately 6 in.

MATERIALS
FOR EACH FLOWER
- 8 sheets of round yellow, orange, or light-green origami paper with white back, 6 in. in diameter

FOLDING INSTRUCTIONS
Anemone Flowers: Flower B
Pages 114–115

1 For each flower, fold 8 petals (Flower B, see pages 114–115) in the same color. Glue them together.

2 Since they are flat on the back, these flowers are ready to use as table decorations.

Variations

For an alternative finish, you can attach a dowel for a stem.

You can also fold the flowers so that the white side is up and the colored sides are facing down.

Beautiful Floating Flowers
decoration for many occasions

FLOWER DIAMETER
approximately 5 in.

MATERIALS
- White waterproof paper, 18 lbs., 8 in. square

FOLDING INSTRUCTIONS
Stamen Flowers: Flowers with a Ring of Stamens (with variation on this page)
Pages 99–102

Cut the sheets of paper into quarters so the flowers do not end up too large.

Tip: Glue the individual petals carefully so that the water will not soak through the bottom of the flowers.

1+2 Fold the square of paper diagonally and reopen. Apply glue as indicated by the white lines in the diagram below and fold the bottom half up again.

3 Fold the left and right corners to the center along the dashed lines, then open them up again.

4 Fold the same corners in, half as far as before.

5 Now fold the two upward-pointing tips down along the dotted lines and back up again.

6+7 Apply glue to the portion marked below and stick it to the other side to form a flower petal. Once several petals are attached together to form a flower, the stamens in the center can be opened.

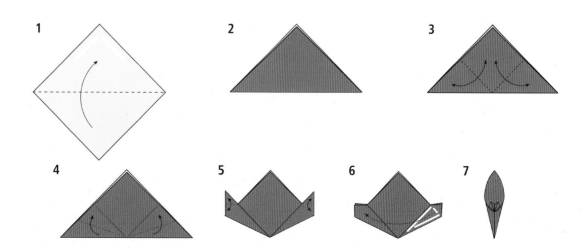

Two-colored Flowers
celebrate pastels

FLOWER DIAMETER
approximately 3½ in.

MATERIALS
FOR EACH FLOWER

- 6 sheets of round origami paper in light yellow and purple (or other pastel color), 4 in. in diameter
- Light-green construction paper
- 16 in. green-paper–covered wire
- Pliers
- Wire cutters
- Pinking shears
- Sewing needle

FOLDING INSTRUCTIONS
Rose Flowers: Flower A; Flower B, Variation 2
Pages 116–118

TEMPLATE
Page 124

1 Fold and glue the purple paper as shown on pages 116–117 for Flower A.

2 Make petals from the yellow paper, following Flower B, Variation 2 (see pages 117–118).

3 Press each purple petal together and trim the edges of the petal to the second fold line with the pinking shears. (The pink flower shown at right is a variation with untrimmed petals.)

4 Make a template for the pair of leaves: Photocopy the pattern on page 124 and enlarge it as specified (for a final length of 6 in.). Glue the photocopy onto a piece of scrap cardboard and cut out the template.

5 Transfer the leaf shape multiple times onto the construction paper and cut out the leaves. Fold each leaf along the two dashed lines and crease with a ruler or pen. Pierce the intersection of the two folded lines with a sewing needle.

6 From the back of the flower, insert the wire into the flower and glue it. Insert the other end of the wire through the hole in the leaf pair; position the leaves farther up the wire and secure them with glue.

Lilac Flowers

beautiful as table decorations

FLOWER DIAMETER
approximately 5 in.

**MATERIALS
FOR EACH FLOWER**
- 3 sheets of batik paper with a vine pattern, 32 lbs., 8 in. square
- 6 black glass beads, $1/10$ in. in diameter
- White pearl bead, $1/2$ in. in diameter
- 12 in. purple aluminum wire, 2 mm in diameter

FOLDING INSTRUCTIONS
Stamen Flowers: Flowers with One Stamen, Flowers with Three Stamens
Pages 99–100

1 Begin by cutting the paper into quarters. Fold twelve petals (with one stamen or with three stamens) for every flower.

2 Glue together six petals to form a flower. Stick another petal in each space between the petals of the inner circle.

3 Finally, glue six beads on the stamens and a pearl bead in the middle.

Tip

- -

Single flowers make a wonderful table decorations. Spread them on the table or lay them on plates. You can also glue them on sturdy colorful wire and place them in a vase.

These hanging flowers are particularly nice with gold beads and gold sepals.

Bending the wire takes some care, but you will be rewarded with a beautiful decoration.

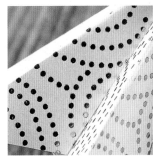

Gilded Hanging Flowers

with curved wire hangers

FLOWER DIAMETER
approximately 4 in.

MATERIALS
FOR EACH
HANGING FLOWER

- 6 or 7 sheets of cream-colored paper with gold polka dots, 4 in. square
- 8½ in. gold aluminum wire, 1 mm in diameter
- Scrap amounts of gold construction paper
- 4 gold bead, $\frac{1}{10}$ to $\frac{1}{4}$ in. in diameter
- One gold bead, ½ in. in diameter

FOLDING INSTRUCTIONS
Festive Flowers: Christmas Roses

Page 111

TEMPLATE
Page 125

1 Using a template, cut a star from the gold construction paper (see page 28). Fold the star along the dotted lines on the template. Punch a hole in the center of the star.

2 Following the directions on page 111 to fold and glue the petals.

3 Press the petals flat.

4 Glue six or seven petals together to form a flower. Before you glue the last pair of petals together, insert the wire through the middle of the flower. Place a small bead at the bottom of the wire and secure it with glue.

5 From the other end of the wire, thread on a small bead, the paper star, a large bead, and another small bead. Bend the long end of the wire into a spiral and place a small bead at the end of the wire. Secure this with glue.

A pair of round-nose pliers will help you bend the wire into an even spiral.

27

Spring Flowers in Shades of Green
delicate and sophisticated

FLOWER DIAMETER
approximately 4 in.

MATERIALS
FOR EACH FLOWER

- 5 sheets of round turquoise origami paper with a vine pattern, 4 in. in diameter
- 16 in. light-green-paper–covered wire
- Light-green construction paper or cardboard
- Rhinestones, ¼ in. in diameter
- Cardboard scraps

FOLDING INSTRUCTIONS
Anemone Flowers: Flower A
Pages 113–114

TEMPLATE
Page 125

1 Fold five petals for each flower (Flower A) and glue them together to form a flower.

2 Make a template for the leaves. Photocopy the pattern from page 125, or trace it with tracing paper; glue the copy of the pattern onto a piece of scrap cardboard and cut out the template. Trace this template several times on the construction paper, then cut out the leaves.

3 Insert the wire into the back of the flower and bend the end at a right angle. To finish, glue the leaves to the wire.

Tip

The flowers shown here can only be laid flat, since the wire is not strong enough to hold them up. If you would like to place the flowers in a vase or a flowerpot, use green aluminum wire about 2 mm in diameter or a thin dowel painted green.

Adorable Snowdrops
simple and beautiful

FLOWER DIAMETER
approximately 10 in.

MATERIALS
- 3 sheets of white origami paper, 4 in. square
- 12 in. green aluminum wire, 2 mm in diameter
- Dark-green wooden bead, ¼ in. in diameter

FOLDING INSTRUCTIONS
Festive Flowers: Christmas Rose, Variation 2 (on this page)
Page 111

Boutonnieres

1 Fold and glue each sheet of paper into a flower petal, following the instructions for Christmas Rose, Variation 2 (see below).

2 Before gluing the third flower petal to the other two, add the wire: Bend the wire, thread on the wooden bead, then insert end of the wire into the flower and secure with glue.

Christmas Rose, Variation 2

Follow the first 12 steps of the Christmas Rose instructions on page 111.

13 Turn the piece over.

14+15 Fold the "kite" tips down along the dotted lines.

16+17 Fold both sides of the kite halves inward. Turn the piece over again.

18 Apply glue to the area marked in yellow and fold the left side to the right to form a petal.

19 When you're ready to assemble the flower, glue this petal to the next by placing glue on the area marked in yellow.

> **Tip**
> Place multiple snowdrops in a vase. You can also place snowdrops in a flowerpot or include them in an arrangement of several different flowers.

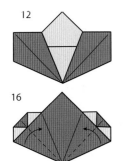
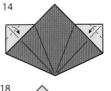
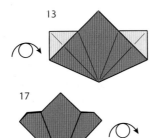
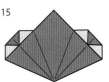

Bright Red Tulips

bright splashes of color with polka dots

FLOWER DIAMETER
approximately 5 in.

MATERIALS
FOR EACH FLOWER
- 5 sheets of red polka dot paper, 4 in. square
- Round wooden dowel, ³/₁₆ in. in diameter, 12 in. long
- Light-green acrylic paint
- Sponge
- Light-green construction paper, 8 by 3 in.

FOLDING INSTRUCTIONS
Calyx Flowers: Flower A
Page 107

TEMPLATE
Page 124

1 Paint the dowel green (this is easiest with a sponge).

2 Fold the construction paper in the middle, the long way, so that it measures 8 by 1½ in. Make a template (see page 28) of the leaf pattern from page 124. Lay the template on the construction paper so that the side with the dashed line is positioned on the fold of the construction paper. Trace the template with a pencil and cut out the leaf. Apply glue to the blunt end of the leaf, on the inside. Place the painted dowel in the folded leaf.

3 Fold five flower petals, following the instructions for Flower A (page 107), and glue them together to form a flower. Glue the top of a dowel inside the flower.

Summery Lilies
great in a flowerpot

FLOWER DIAMETER
approximately 3 in.

MATERIALS
FOR EACH FLOWER

- Yellow, orange, or red paper, 18 lbs., 4 in. square
- Light- or dark-green paper, 6 in. square
- Round wooden dowel, 3/16 in. in diameter, 6 in. long
- Adhesive putty

FOLDING INSTRUCTIONS
Lily Flowers: Flowers A and B
Pages 103–104

1 Take a small sheet of paper and fold a Flower A, following the directions on pages 103–104. Take the large sheet of green paper and fold a Flower B. Cut off the ends of both flowers so that the flowers can be placed on the dowel.

2 Take a piece of adhesive putty and form a small ball (about ¼ in. in diameter); press it on the end of the dowel. Put the end of the dowel through the bottom of the colored flower and press it upward until the adhesive putty reaches the center of the flower. Pinch the flower a bit to stick it securely to the dowel.

3 Take more of the adhesive putty and form a sausage-like shape about ½ in. long. Place this around the dowel, about 1½ in. from the other end. Insert the dowel into the second flower until the adhesive clay reaches the center of the flower. Align the flower so the petals are staggered with the those of the top flower, then gently pinch the center of the flower to stick it to the dowel.

Tip

You can make this flower springy, summery, or Christmassy. Whatever the occasion, adding variation to these flowers can give your decorated table a unique look.

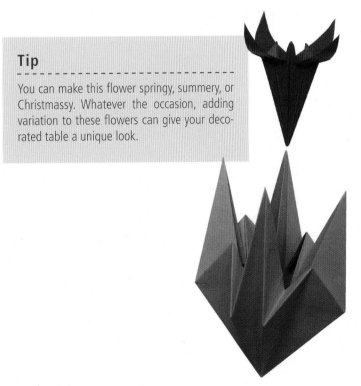

Enchanting Flower Stars
beautiful in red and gold

FLOWER DIAMETER
approximately 8 in.

MATERIALS
- 16 sheets of two-sided origami paper (gold and red) with a star pattern, 6 in.

FOLDING INSTRUCTIONS
Festive Flowers: Winter Aconite; Christmas Rose, Variation 1 (on this page)

Pages 111–112

1 Take eight sheets of the colored paper. Fold and glue them, gold side facing inwards, into wintry flower petals (see pages 111–112). Press the eight flower petals flat. Glue the petals together to form the inner star.

2 Take the other eight sheets of paper. With the red side facing inwards, fold and glue them into flower petals, following the instructions for the Christmas Rose Variation 1 (see below).

3 Glue the red petals around the inner star, between each pair of points.

Christmas Rose, Variation 1

Follow the first twelve steps of the Christmas Rose instructions (see page 111).

13+14 Fold the points inward along the dotted lines.

15 Fold the outer sides inward.

16 Place glue on the right triangle (marked with a yellow line) and fold the left side over to the right to form a petal.

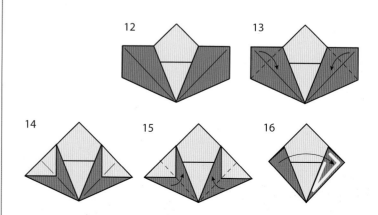

FLOWER SPHERES

Flower balls are the highest form of floragami. In order to create these impressive pieces of art, you need patience and practice. The end results are well worth the effort!

Dots over Dots

cheerful and cute

SPHERE DIAMETER
approximately 8½ in.

MATERIALS

- 21 sheets of green paper, 18 lbs., 6 in. square
- 20 sheets of purple paper with polka dots, 18 lbs., 6 in. square

FOLDING INSTRUCTIONS
Lily Flowers: Flower A, Simple Lily Sphere
Pages 103–105

1 Fold twenty lilies from the green and yellow paper, following the instructions on pages 103–104.

2 From the remaining sheet of green paper, cut out four circles 1¾ in. in diameter. Fold these pieces according to the directions on page 104.

3 Glue four green lilies to each of the four circles from step 2. Follow the basic instructions on pages 104–105 to put them together.

4 Glue the rest of the four green flowers in the spaces of the sphere. Insert the violet flowers into the green flowers and glue them in place.

Tip

The spheres will look very stylish made with red paper with white dots. Instead of green paper for the bases of the flowers, try white paper—or make it the other way around, with white flowers in red bases.

White Christmas Rose Spheres

gorgeous, elegant decorations

SPHERE DIAMETER
without greens: approximately 6 in.
with greens: approximately 8 in.

MATERIALS
- 60 sheets of white origami paper, 4 in. square
- Dark-green construction paper
- 30 in. pink crochet thread

FOLDING INSTRUCTIONS
Festive Flowers: Christmas Roses, Festive Flower Spheres

Pages 111–113

TEMPLATE
Page 124

1 Make twelve flowers, each with five petals, following the directions for the Christmas Rose (page 111).

2 Put the flowers together as described on page 112 to form a flower sphere.

3 From the construction paper, cut out ninety single leaves using the leaf pattern from page 124. Glue the leaves together in threes, forming a fanlike shape; you should end up with thirty of these shapes in all. Place each "fan" in one of the thirty openings of the sphere and glue in place.

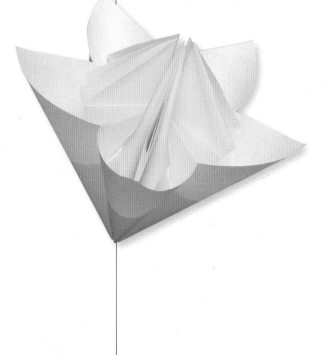

Dramatic Double Flowers

simple spheres in shades of red

SPHERE DIAMETER

approximately 4 in.

MATERIALS

- 10 sheets of pink or maroon round origami paper, 4 in in diameter
- 1 flat purple faceted bead for each flower, ½ in. in diameter
- 2 maroon acrylic beads for each flower, ¹⁄₁₀ to ¼ in. in diameter
- 20 in. pink crochet thread

FOLDING INSTRUCTIONS

Anemone Flowers: Flower C, Variation (on this page)

Page 115

1 Make twenty petals for each sphere. Assemble ten of the petals into a flower. Before you glue the last petal in place, insert a piece of crochet thread with a round bead tied at the end into the middle of the flower and glue in place. (You should end up with an upside-down half-sphere hanging from a length of thread, with a bead at the bottom.)

2 Glue the petals of the second flower together, building the flower around the thread, above the first half-sphere. The points of the two flowers should interlock to form a sphere. Make sure that the tips of the petals of the two flowers alternate.

3 To finish the sphere, thread the faceted bead and the round bead onto the thread at the top of the sphere.

Tip

You can also work with eleven or twelve petals for the flowers. What is important is that the two flowers have the same number of petals.

Flower C, Variation

1 Follow the directions for Flower C on page 115 up to step 6 (do not glue the petal). Fold point E around point D. Press together, apply glue where marked with a yellow line, and press together again.

2 Repeat this on the opposite side with points C and B.

3 Open the middle right protruding fold, apply glue where marked with a yellow line, and press together. The flower petal is now finished.

4 To assemble the finished petals into a flower, apply glue to the small folded part on one side (marked in yellow below), place another petal next to it, and press them firmly together. Continue gluing the petals together; when you get to the last one, glue it to the first petal.

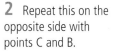

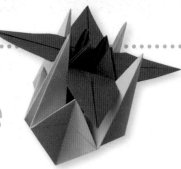

Heavenly Flowers in Blue

delightfully fresh and summery

SPHERE DIAMETER

approximately 6½ in.

MATERIALS

- 14 sheets each of light-blue and dark-blue paper, 18 lbs., 4 in. square
- 2 dark-blue wooden beads, ¼ in. in diameter
- Light-blue plastic bead, ½ in. in diameter
- Blue teardrop faceted bead, 1¼ in. long and ¾ in. wide
- Dark-blue crochet thread, around 1 yd. long

FOLDING INSTRUCTIONS

Lily Flowers: Flowers A and B, Lily Star Spheres
Pages 103–104, 106

1 Fold the light-blue sheets of paper into fourteen Flower Bs, following the directions on page 103. Press each flower together so that it has a cross shape when viewed from above (photos 1 and 2, below). Glue six of these flowers together around a length of thread to form a star (see page 106).

2 Make fourteen Flower As from the dark-blue paper (see pages 103–104 and photo 3, below). Glue six dark-blue lilies inside the six flowers of the light-blue star. Glue the remaining dark-blue lilies inside the remaining light-blue lilies (see photo 4). Glue four of these double flowers on the star to form a half-sphere. Turn the half-sphere over and attach the remaining four double flowers to finish the sphere.

3 Thread the beads onto the length of thread extended below the ball, as shown in the photo. Tie a double knot to keep the beads in place. Finally, tie the large faceted gem to the end of the thread.

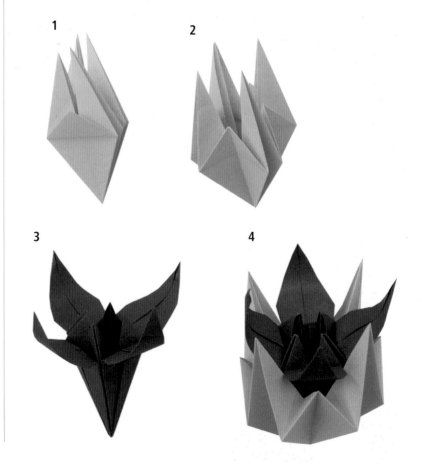

1

2

3

4

Spectacular Eye-Catchers
a flower sphere to display outdoors

SPHERE DIAMETER
approximately 7½ in.

MATERIALS
- 24 sheets of green polka-dot weatherproof paper, 6 in. square
- 24 sheets white and green patterned weatherproof paper, 6 in. square

FOLDING INSTRUCTIONS
Garden Flowers: Two-Part Flower
Pages 122–123

Individual Flower

1   A single flower consists of four inner petals and four outer petals. Follow the directions on page 122, but omit step 3 so the inner petals have rounded petals. For the inner flower petals, use the white patterned paper. For the outer petals, use the green polka dot paper.

2   First glue the four inner flower petals into a flower; then glue the four outer flower petals between these the inner ones.

Flower Sphere

A flower sphere consists of six individual flowers. Glue three individual flowers together to form a half-sphere; then repeat with the other three. You should now have two half-spheres. Glue the two half-spheres together back to back. (For exact instructions with step-by-step photos on how to form the flower sphere, see page 123).

> **Tip**
>
> Paint a small dowel with water-resistant paint and glue the end of it inside the sphere as you assemble it. Stick the finished flower sphere in the ground or a pot.

Christmassy Flower Spheres

beautiful decoration for the holidays

SPHERE DIAMETER

approximately 8½ in.

MATERIALS

- 60 sheets of two-sided paper (dark red and dark green), 18 lbs., 6 in.
- 12 dark-red pearl beads, ¼ in. in diameter
- 2 dark-green wooden beads, ¼ in. in diameter
- 1 red wooden bead, ½ in. in diameter
- Four pieces of dark-red crochet thread, 1 yd. (to hang the sphere), 65 ft. (for tassel), 20 in. (to tie off the tassel), and 8 in. (to attach the tassel)

FOLDING INSTRUCTIONS

Stamen Flowers: Flowers with a Ring of Stamens, Stamen Flower Sphere

Pages 99–102

Tip

Use individual flowers to decorate your dinner table, mantel, or Christmas greens.

---

1 Make sixty individual petals, following the instructions on pages 99–101. Glue these petals together in fives to create a total of twelve flowers.

2 Glue the flowers together to form a sphere (see pages 101–102), gluing a length of crochet thread through the middle of the sphere as you assemble it.

3 If you like, you can glue beads in the centers of the flowers. Thread three beads (green, red, and green again) on the length of thread at the bottom of the sphere.

Make a Tassel

1 Wrap the longest piece of crochet thread fifty times around a book about 8 in. wide. Tie off the top of the loop formed with the 1-yard length of thread and slide the thread off the book.

2 Make a loop from the 20-inch piece of thread and lay it on top of the tassel, near the tied-off end, with the short end of the loop toward the top.

3 Bring the long end of the loop around the back of the tassel and back to the front. Keep wrapping this end around the tassel smoothly, covering up the loop as you go.

4 Pull the end of the loop thread through the bottom of the loop.

5 Pull the beginning of the loop thread tight, until the bottom edge of the loop disappears under the thread you wound around the tassel.

6 Cut off both ends of the loop thread. Then trim a small amount off the bottom of the tassel.

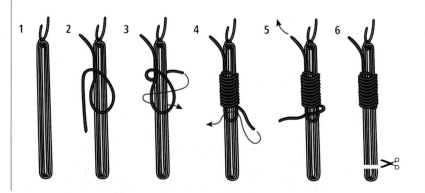

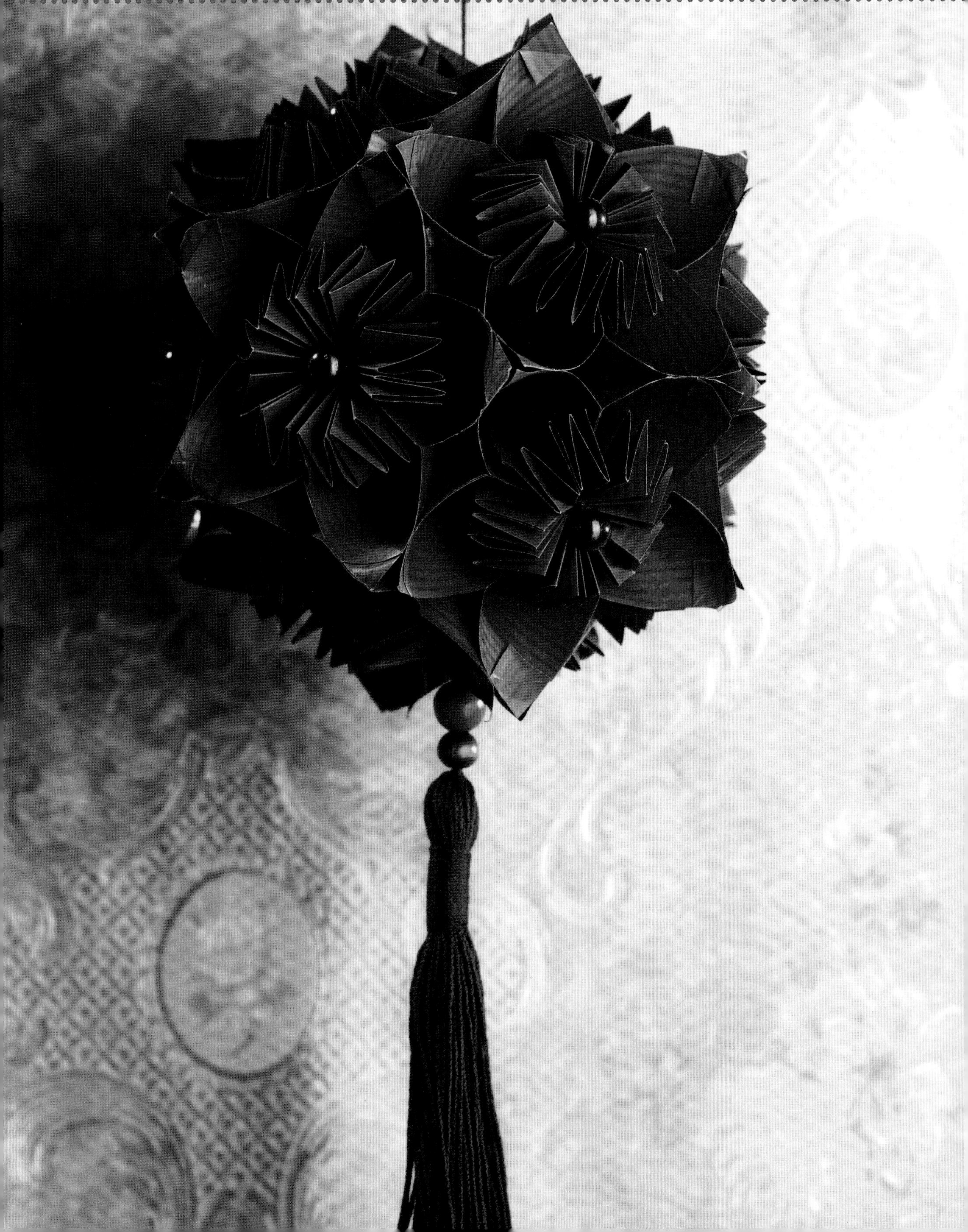

Spring Lilies

with fresh and bright colors

SPHERE DIAMETER
approximately 5½ in.

MATERIALS
- 5 sheets of light-green paper, 18 lbs., 4 in.
- Four sheets each of dark-green, light-yellow, dark-yellow, and light orange paper, 18 lbs., 4 in. square
- Light-green crochet thread, around 1 yd. long
- 4 dark-green wooden beads, $\frac{1}{10}$ in. in diameter
- 4 light-yellow wooden beads, ¼ in. in diameter
- 2 green faceted beads, ½ in. in diameter

FOLDING INSTRUCTIONS
Lily Flowers: Flower A, Simple Lily Spheres
Pages 103–105

1 Fold four lilies in each color, following the instructions on pages 103–104.

2 Cut four circles 1 in. wide from the remaining light-green paper. Fold these pieces according to the instructions on page 104.

3 Glue four lilies (one in every color) to each light-green circle. Following the instructions on pages 104–105, assemble the flowers into a sphere; glue a thread through the middle of the sphere as you build it. Try to avoid placing two same-colored lilies next to one another. Use the remaining four flowers to fill in the gaps at the end.

4 Thread beads on the thread at the bottom of the sphere, as pictured at right; secure the beads with knots and a little glue.

> **Tip**
>
> These spheres also look beautiful in mixed pastel colors—for example, in pink, light blue, light green, light orange, and lilac. Try out different color combinations.

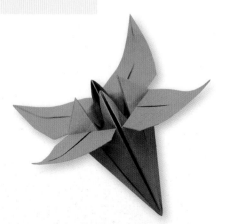

Dreams of Turquoise
spectacular and springlike

SPHERE DIAMETER
approximately 12 in.

MATERIALS
- 60 sheets of patterned turquoise paper, 6 in. square
- Nylon thread, about 1 yd. long
- Wooden or plastic blue bead, ¼ in. in diameter

FOLDING INSTRUCTIONS
Calyx Flowers: Flower B, Variation 2 (using ¼ in. wide angle template); Twelve-Flower Sphere
Pages 107–108, 110

TEMPLATE
Page 125

1 Fold sixty petals, following the first six steps of the instructions for Flower B (page 107). In step 2, apply a small amount of glue beneath the triangle before folding it in.

2 Continue with the instructions below for Flower B Variation.

3 Assemble the flowers into a sphere following the twelve-flower sphere instructions on page 110.

Flower B, Variation 2
Fold Flower B and stop at step 6.

7 Fold the right corner to the middle and then back.

8+9 Repeat this fold on the left side, then unfold both sides all the way.

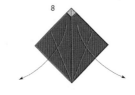

10, 11+12 Fold the right corner in along the dashed line, then fold the tip of it back.

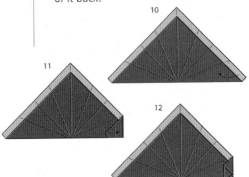

13 Repeat steps 10–12 on the left side. Fold both sides up along the dashed lines.

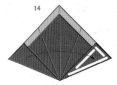

14 Apply glue on the piece where indicated by the white lines. Fold the left half to the right. The flower petal is finished.

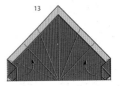

15 To attach the petals together, glue them on the lower portion, where indicated below by the white lines. Put the petals together in sets of five.

Pink Flower Spheres
romantic and delicate

SPHERE DIAMETER
approximately 8½ in.

MATERIALS
- 60 sheets of pink paper with red polka dots on one side, 18 lbs., 6 in. square

FOLDING INSTRUCTIONS
Stamen Flowers: Flowers with One Stamen, Stamen Flower Spheres
Pages 99–102

1 Make twelve flowers with five petals each, following the instructions on pages 99–101.

2 Follow the directions on pages 101–102 to assemble the flowers into a sphere.

Tip

This flower sphere will also look nice made with paper with different colored polka dots.

The individual flower petals interlock to form a beautiful flower sphere.

Lilac Spheres

delicate as a spring breeze

SPHERE DIAMETER

approximately 6 in.

MATERIALS

FOR EACH SPHERE

- 12 sheets each of white and lilac round origami paper, 4 in. in diameter
- Clear, lilac, or white plastic bead, $\frac{1}{10}$ to $\frac{1}{4}$ in. in diameter
- 24 in. nylon thread

FOLDING INSTRUCTIONS

Anemone Flowers: Flower C

Page 115

1 Fold the twenty-four sheets of origami paper into flower petals (Flower C), following the instructions on page 115; glue them together to form two flowers of different colors. Thread a small bead on the nylon thread and secure it with a knot. Thread the other end of the thread through the center opening of the paper flower and pull the bead into the bottom of the opening (to ensure that the flower hangs evenly).

2 Now take the second flower, thread onto the thread above the first one, and position it so that the petals of the flowers interlock.

3 Take another bead and thread it on above the second flower, pressing it into the top opening of the flower to keep it hanging evenly.

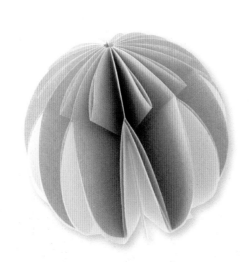

Pretty in Pink

transform baking cups into a beautiful flower

SPHERE DIAMETER
approximately 5 in.

MATERIALS
FOR EACH FLOWER
- 24 patterned pink paper baking cups, 2 in. in diameter (bottom)

FOLDING INSTRUCTIONS
Rose Flowers: Flower B, Variation 1; Rose Flower Spheres
Pages 117–120

1 Fold the twenty-four flower petals following the instructions for Flower B, Variation 1, on pages 117–118. Let the glue dry for at least an hour before continuing to work with the flower.

2 Glue the flower petals together in fours to form flowers. You will have a total of six flowers. Let the glue dry again.

3 Assemble the individual flowers into a sphere, following the instructions on pages 119–120.

Tip: Note also the introduction on working with baking cups on page 116.

Romantic Doilies
in deep, rich red

SPHERE DIAMETER
approximately 6½ in.

MATERIALS
- 24 red paper doilies, 6 in. in diameter

FOLDING INSTRUCTIONS
Rose Flowers: Flower B, Rose Flower Spheres
Pages 117–120

1 Please note the tips on working with doilies on page 116. For the sphere, fold twenty-four flower petals, following the instructions for flower B on pages 117–118. Let the glue dry for at least an hour before continuing to work.

2 Glue the flower petals together in fours to form flowers. You will have six flowers in all. Let the glue dry again.

3 Assemble the six individual flowers into a flower sphere, following the instructions on pages 119–120.

Summery Decorations
made with two-tone flowers

SPHERE DIAMETER
approximately 9 in.

MATERIALS
- 24 sheets of two-sided origami paper, 6 in. square

FOLDING INSTRUCTIONS
Calyx Flowers: Flower C, Variation 1 (on this page); Six-Flower Spheres
Pages 108–109

TEMPLATE
Page 125

1 Work steps 1–3 and step 5 of the instructions for flower C (page 108). Omitting step 4 yields a rounded petal.

2 Proceed with steps 6–11, below, for the variation.

3 Combine the flowers to form a six-flowered sphere. The directions for assembling the sphere are on page 109.

Calyx Flower Variation C

Follow the instructions for Flower C until step 6, omitting step 4 (see page 108).

6 Fold the right corner up to the fold line, then unfold it.

7, 8+9 Fold the right corner to the new fold line. Then fold this part up once more.

10 Repeat steps 5–9 on the left side. Apply glue to the bottom folded part (marked with white lines) and fold the sides together.

11 Fold the stamens on the dotted lines. The flower petal is now finished. To assemble the flowers, apply glue to the bottom of each petal, as marked by the white lines, to the bottom folded piece; put four petals together to form a flower.

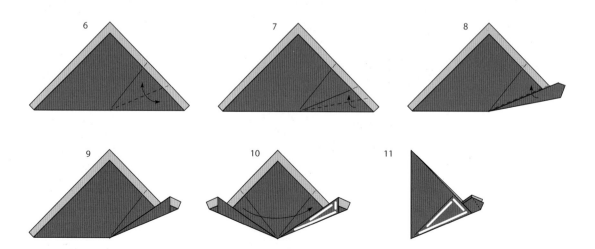

Beaded Flower Spheres

a great gift for romantics

SPHERE DIAMETER
approximately 6 in.

MATERIALS

- 60 sheets of pink paper, 18 lbs., 4 in. square
- 14 black wooden beads, ¼ in. in diameter
- Dark pink round faceted bead, ½ in. in diameter
- Dark pink teardrop-shaped faceted bead, 1½ in. long by ¾ in. wide
- 30 in. black crochet thread

FOLDING INSTRUCTIONS
Stamen Flowers: Flowers with Three Stamens; Stamen Flower Sphere

Pages 99–102

1   Fold each sheet of origami paper in a petal with three stamens (see instructions on pages 99–100). Glue the petals together in sets of five to form twelve flowers.

2   Assemble the twelve flowers, as described on pages 101–102, to form a sphere. Glue a length of thread through the middle of the sphere as you put it together, leaving a length extending beyond the sphere at the top and bottom.

3   Glue a wooden bead to the center of each flower. Thread a wooden bead, the round faceted bead, and the remaining wooden bead on the thread at the bottom of the sphere. Tie a double knot below them to hold them in place, with the top bead about ½ in. below the flowers. Trim the thread to the desired length (here, about 1 in. beyond the lower wooden bead) and tie the teardrop bead at the end.

Tip

Instead of the constrasting black thread and black beads, you can use beads and thread in a shade of pink. This will give the sphere a softer look.

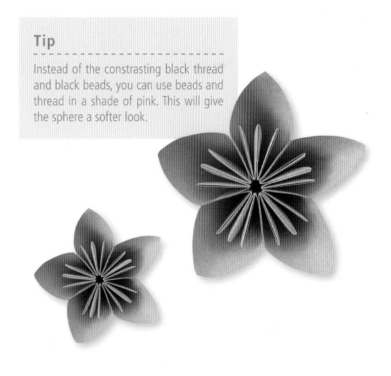

Classy and Festive

flower decorations for the holiday season

SPHERE DIAMETER

with leaves: approximately 10½ in.

without leaves: approximately 10 in.

MATERIALS

- 60 sheets of gold and cream paper patterned with vines and small stars, 6 in. square
- Gold construction paper
- Gold lurex cord
- 12 gold beads, ½ in. in diameter

FOLDING INSTRUCTIONS

Festive Flowers: Winter Aconites; Festive Flower Spheres

Pages 111–113

TEMPLATE

Page 125

1 Fold sixty petals and assemble them into twelve five-petal flowers, following the Wintry Flower folding instructions on pages 111–112. Glue a gold bead between the stamens of each flower (optional).

2 Assemble the flowers into a sphere, following the instructions on pages 112–113; glue the hanging thread in the middle of the sphere as you put it together.

3 Trace the leaf shape from page 125 and make a template (see page 28). Trace the template sixty times on construction paper and cut out the leaves. Crease each leaf down the middle line. Glue the leaves together in pairs, then glue the pairs in the gaps between the flowers in the sphere.

FANCY FLOWER DECORATIONS

Not only are there countless variations of folding techniques and paper choices, you can also use floragami flowers in many different ways. The following pages present some alternate ways of folding and decorating with floragami.

Winter Aconites in Bright Yellow

beautiful solo or in a flower chain

FLOWER DIAMETER
approximately 4 in.

MATERIALS
FOR EACH FLOWER

- 6 sheets of yellow paper, 4 in. square
- Dark-green construction paper, 5 by 7 in.
- 8 in. green aluminum wire, 2 mm in diameter

ADDITIONAL MATERIALS
FOR THE FLOWER
CHAIN

- 1 green wooden bead, ¼ in. in diameter
- 1 yellow wooden bead, ¹⁄₁₀ in. in diameter
- 20 in. dark-green crochet thread

FOLDING INSTRUCTIONS
Festive Flowers: Winter Aconites
Pages 111–112

TEMPLATE
Page 124

Flower with Stem

1 Fold the construction paper for the leaves in half widthwise. Trace the leaf template from page 124, then lay it on the construction paper so the dashed line is along the fold line. Trace the template, then cut out the shape. Open the leaf piece and pierce the middle with a pin.

2 Fold and glue the six sheets of origami paper into petals, following the instructions for the Winter Aconite on pages 111–112. Glue the petals together to form a flower, inserting the wire into the middle before you glue the sixth petal in place. Thread the wire through the hole in the leaf piece and glue it to the base of the flower.

Flower Hanger

1 Make the flower petals and leaf pieces as described at left for the single flower.

2 Tie a wooden bead at one end of a length of yarn. Thread on a leaf piece, then assemble a flower with the yarn through the center. Thread a small yellow bead onto the yarn and slide it down between the flower's stamens.

3 Thread a green bead onto the yarn. Position the bead about 3 in. above the flower and bring the yarn around the bead and thread it through again from bottom to top, so that the bead stays in place on the yarn. Thread on another leaf piece above the bead, then assemble another flower around the yarn as before. Continue until the string is your desired length.

Welcome Spring!

distinctive blossoms with pinked edges

FLOWER DIAMETER
approximately 4 in.

MATERIALS
FOR EACH FLOWER

- 6 sheets each of white and green round origami paper, 4 in. in diameter
- 4 clear bicone beads, $\frac{1}{10}$ in. in diameter
- 1 clear faceted bead, $\frac{1}{2}$ in. in diameter
- 2 green faceted beads, $\frac{1}{4}$ in. in diameter
- 24 in. white crochet thread

FOLDING INSTRUCTIONS
Anemone Flowers: Flowers A and C
Pages 113–115

1 Thread a green faceted bead and three small clear bicone beads on the crochet thread. Tie a double or triple knot below the beads so they do not move.

2 Fold six green sheets (Flower A) and six white sheets (Flower C) into petals, following the instructions on pages 113–115. For a special effect, you can trim the edges of the white petals with pinking shears. Glue the petals together into a flower, alternating between green and white petals.

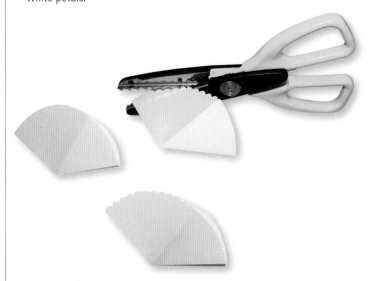

3 Insert the thread through the middle of the flower before gluing the last petal to the first. Thread a clear faceted bead, a green faceted bead, and a clear bicone bead onto the thread above the flower.

String of Flower Lights

great for summer parties!

FLOWER DIAMETER
approximately 5 in.

MATERIALS
- 60 sheets of yellow and turquoise patterned paper, 4 in. square
- String of LED lights with 10 bulbs

FOLDING INSTRUCTIONS
Garden Flowers: Simple Flowers with Variation (on this page)
Page 121

1 Fold six flower petals for each flower, following the instructions below and on page 121. Glue the six petals for each flower together, checking that the opening in the middle is large enough for the LED light to fit through. If the opening is too small, cut a little more off the bases of the other petals.

2 Place the ten flowers carefully on the lights.

Garden Flower, Variation

Begin by following steps 1–12 of the instructions for Garden Flowers on page 121. Continue with steps 13d-15d, below. Finish the petals by working steps 16e-19e.

13d Fold both of the corners up along the red dashed lines and then back again.

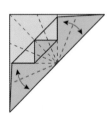

14d Fold both corners up to the fold line just made.

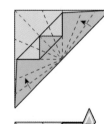

15d Spread glue on the right folded piece (outlined in yellow) and fold the left half to meet it.

16e+17e Fold the stamens up to the inside as shown below.

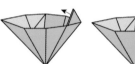

18e Cut off the bottom tip of the flower (along the red line).

19e Glue the six flower petals together to form one flower, applying glue on the area outlined in yellow.

Decorative Flower Wreath

in pink and red

FLOWER DIAMETER
approximately 3½ in.

MATERIALS
- 18 sheets of pink and red round origami paper, 4 in. in diameter
- Small amount of light-green cardboard or posterboard
- 6 roofing nails with ¼ in. heads, ¾ in. long
- Pinking shears (round serrated edge)

FOLDING INSTRUCTIONS
Rose Flowers: Flower B

Pages 117–118

TEMPLATE
Page 124

1 Photocopy the pattern for the wreath base, enlarging it 250 percent for a diameter of 8 in.

2 Glue the photocopy on a piece of scrap cardboard and cut out the shape to make a template. Trace the template on the green cardboard. Mark the locations for the roofing nails by piercing the template with a needle at the six points marked with small circles. Cut out the wreath base.

3 Push the roofing nails through the wreath base from the bottom up at the marked spots.

4 Fold and glue the sheets of origami paper into flower petals, following the instructions for Flower B (see pages 117–118). Flatten the petals and cut from the top to the second fold line with the pinking shears.

5 Glue six petals of the same color together to form a flower. Once you have assembled all six flowers, place the flowers on the wreath, with the roofing nails in their centers.

Variation

The instructions above produce a wreath that is stable enough to use as a table decoration. However, if you would like to hang the wreath, it needs to be stronger. You can strengthen the wreath by adding a second layer of carboard on the base. Attach the flowers to the wreath with hot glue.

Cloud of Lilacs

delicate and elegant

SPHERE DIAMETER
approximately 8 in.

MATERIALS
- 30 sheets of paper with a lilac floral print and white back, 4 in. square

FOLDING INSTRUCTIONS
Calyx Flowers: Flower C; Half Spheres
Pages 108, 110

1 Fold the petals and glue them together in groups of five to form flowers, following the instructions on page 108. You do not need an angle template, but leave a margin of about ⅛ in. along the edge when you make the first fold.

2 Glue together the six flowers together to form a half sphere as described on page 110.

Variations

Lighted Decoration The half sphere is especially eye-catching when placed on a plate with a string of LED lights underneath.

Full Sphere You can also glue two half spheres together to form a full sphere of twelve flowers. Display it by hanging it from a thread or placing it on a dish.

Harmony in Blue
a flower wreath for the table

WREATH DIAMETER
approximately 12 in.

MATERIALS
- Light-blue poster board, 8 in. square
- 18 sheets of light blue and dark blue round origami paper, 4 in. in diameter

FOLDING INSTRUCTIONS
Anemone Flowers: Flower A
Pages 113–114

1 First, create the base of the wreath. Find the center of the cardboard square by marking both diagonals with a pencil and ruler; the point where the lines cross in the middle is the center. Use a compass to draw two circles around this center point, one 3 in. in diameter, and one 3½ in. Cut around both circles to get a cardboard ring.

2 Make three light blue flowers and three dark blue flowers, each with six petals, following the directions on pages 113–114.

3 Arrange all the flowers on the cardboard ring. Once you have them positioned the way you want, glue them into place.

Spray of Flowers in Yellow and White

an enchanting table decoration

SPHERE DIAMETER
approximately 8 in.

MATERIALS
- 50 sheets of origami paper, 4 in. square (example made with 20 in light yellow, 15 in yellow, and 15 in white)

FOLDING INSTRUCTIONS
Calyx Flowers: Flower A;
Half Spheres
Pages 107 and 110

Tip: You can put two half spheres together to form a full sphere. Using plenty of glue, attach a hanging thread to one of the half spheres. When the glue is dry, glue the two spheres together, using clothespins to hold them together while the glue dries. If there are gaps in the sphere, you can fold more flowers and glue them in the gaps.

1   Fold the flower petals, following the instructions for Flower A (see page 107). Assemble the petals in groups of five to form ten flowers.

2+3   Lay seven flowers on the table in the shape or a ring. Make sure that you do not have two flowers of the same color next to each other. Glue the flowers together where they touch.

4   Glue on the eighth flower on top of the ring of seven flowers.

5   Glue on the ninth and tenth flowers. The half-sphere is now finished. If you like, you can glue beads to the middles of the flowers.

Bottom view of the half sphere.

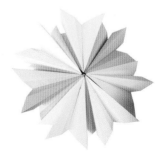

Orange Light Chain

for romantic moments

FLOWER DIAMETER

approximately 3½ in.

MATERIALS

- 50 sheets of orange round origami paper, 4 in. in diameter
- Thick red marker
- String of LED lights with 10 bulbs

FOLDING INSTRUCTIONS

Rose Flowers: Flower A, Variation 3 (on this page)

Page 116

1 Cover the work area with newspaper, as the marker may bleed through the origami paper.

2 Place a sheet of paper on the work area and outline the edge all the way around with the thick marker to produce a border about about ⅛ in. wide. The color will bleed through the paper so that the line is visible on the back as well. Add borders to the other sheets in the same way (moving to a different area on the newspaper each time to avoid ink from previous sheets bleeding into the current one).

Flower A, Variation 3

Start with steps 1 to 4 of Flower A (page 116).

5 Fold up the two bottom corners along the red lines, then fold them back down again.

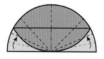

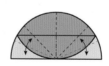

6 and 7 Then fold the corners up to the fold lines just made.

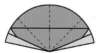

8 and 9 Apply glue on the folded flap on the right (marked with yellow lines) and fold the left half over to the right. The first flower petal is now finished.

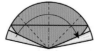

3 Fold the flowers, following the instructions for Flower A, Variation 3 (below).

4 Glue the petals together in fives to form flowers; attach each flower to one of the bulbs of the string of lights.

10 Bring the glued part in to the middle of the petal to make space for the bulb, folding it in along the existing fold lines (marked in red).

11 Cut off a piece at the bottom with the scissors (red line). To ensure that the same amount is cut off for each petal, use the first petal as a template for the others. To test it out, assemble a flower and put a bulb in it. If the opening does not fit, cut off more or less from the rest of the flower petals.

12 To assemble the flowers, apply glue on the area outlined in yellow and glue the flower petals together.

Clever Flower Hanger
the blossoms fit together like a puzzle

FLOWER DIAMETER
approximately 4 in.

MATERIALS
FOR EACH HANGER

- Round origami paper, 4 in. in diameter: for white variation, 14 sheets; for light-yellow variation, 10 sheets; for light-orange variation, 13 sheets; for cream variation, 7 sheets
- Clear faceted beads, 1 bead ¾ to 1 in. in diameter (for light-orange, white, and light-yellow variations), plus 2 beads ½ in. in diameter for light-orange variation
- 4 clear plastic beads, ¹⁄₁₀ to ¼ in. in diameter
- 24 in. nylon thread
- Cardboard scrap

FOLDING INSTRUCTIONS
Anemone Flowers: Flower C

Page 115

TEMPLATE
Page 124

Tip: The flower hanger is made of two identical flowers that are put together to form a sphere; the tips of the petals interlock with one another. The white hanger pictured on the opposite page (made from two flowers) is identical to the cream-colored hanger (except that the cream-colored one has only one flower). The light yellow hanger is made of flowers with five petals and the light orange hanger has six petals.

1   Fold the required number of flower petals (see materials list), following the directions on page 115. Do not glue them together yet.

2   Trace the template from page 124, glue it on the cardboard, and cut it out. Lay this stencil on the folded flower petal and trace around it with a pencil. Cut along this line, then glue the petals together to form flowers.

3   On one end of the nylon thread, tie a small plastic bead and pull the other end through a flower. If the hanger will be made of only one flower, the rounded end of the flower should be at the top; for a hanger made of two flowers, thread the first flower with the rounded end down. Thread one to three faceted beads onto the thread before finally threading the other flower on with the rounded end up.

Double Spheres
beautiful window decorations

FLOWER DIAMETER
approximately 4 in.

MATERIALS
- 24 sheets of green or brown round paper with floral print, 4 in. in diameter
- Clear faceted beads, ½ and ¾ in. in diameter
- 4 clear plastic beads, ¹⁄₁₀ to ¼ in. in diameter
- 24 in. nylon thread

FOLDING INSTRUCTIONS
Anemone Flowers: Flower A

Pages 113–114

1 Fold the twenty-four petals according to the instructions on page 113–114 (Flower A) and assemble them into two flowers.

2 Tie a small knot at one end of the nylon thread. The central opening of these flowers has a diameter of about ¼ in., large enough that the flowers will hang a bit crooked on their own. To fix this, thread on a plastic bead about the diameter of the opening, then thread on the flower, pressing the bead into the opening. Add another small bead and press it into the opening at the top of the flower. Now the first flower should hang straight.

3 Thread on the large faceted bead. Then add the second paper flower, with a bead before and after it, as on the first flower.

Delicate Paper Lantern Flowers
in romantic blue

FLOWER DIAMETER
approximately 5½ in.

MATERIALS
FOR EVERY FLOWER
- 5 light-blue paper doilies, 6 in. in diameter
- 3 light-blue plastic beads, ¼ in. in diameter
- Clear faceted bead, ½ in. in diameter
- Light-blue crochet thread

FOLDING INSTRUCTIONS
Rose Flowers: Flower A
Pages 116–117

Tip: Make sure to read the information about working with doilies on page 116.

1 Fold five flower petals, following the directions for Flower A on pages 116–117.

2 Let the glue dry before gluing the petals together to form a flower. Before gluing the last petal on the first one to comple the flower, insert the crochet thread through the middle of the flower so it extends past the flower on both ends.

3 At the lower end of the hanger thread, attach a bead. To do this, tie a few knots in the the thread, apply some glue, and push the bead over the knots.

4 When the glue is dry, thread a plastic bead, a glass bead, and another plastic bead on the other end of the thread.

Tip

- -

You could also make these flowers with seven petals instead of five. It also looks nice when you hang multiple flowers on the same thread. In between the flowers just string on more beads.

Playful Christmas Flowers
in modern colors

FLOWER DIAMETER
approximately 5 in.

MATERIALS
- 5 sheets of paper with a purple and white star pattern, 6 in. square
- Purple crochet thread
- 6 or 7 purple plastic beads, 1/10 in. in diameter
- 2 purple star beads, 1/4 and 1/2 in. in diameter

FOLDING INSTRUCTIONS
Festive Flowers: Christmas Roses, Variation 3 (on this page)
Page 111

TEMPLATE
Page 125

1 Attach a bead on one end of the crochet thread.

2 Fold four of the sheets of paper into petals, following the instructions for the Christmas Rose, Variation 3 (see below). Assemble them into a flower, placing the thread with the bead through the middle of the flower before gluing the last two petals together. Thread five or six beads onto the thread above the flower for spacers.

3 Cut out the sepal star from the fifth sheet of paper (the pattern is on page 125). Fold it as indicated on the pattern so the purple side is up.

4 Thread the sepal star, a round bead, then both of the star beads onto the thread above the flower.

Christmas Rose, Variation 3

Begin by following the first twelve steps for the Christmas Rose on page 111.

12+13 Turn the piece over.

14+15 Fold both kite-shaped side pieces in half inwards. Turn the piece over again.

16 Apply glue to the area outlined in yellow and fold the left side to the right to form a flower petal.

17 To glue the petals together, apply glue to the area outlined in yellow below.

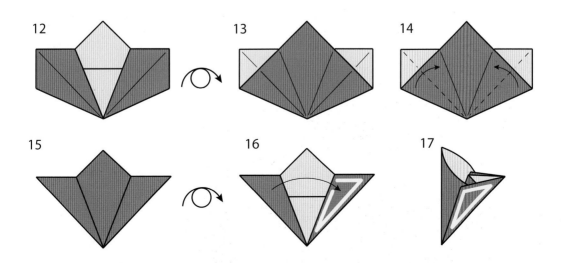

Transparent and Elegant

hanging flowers in black and white

FLOWER DIAMETER
approximately 4 in.

MATERIALS
FOR EACH FLOWER

- White semitransparent paper with a black vine pattern, 31 lbs.
- 2 black wooden beads, ¼ in. in diameter
- 1 clear glass bead, ½ in. in diameter
- 30 in. black crochet thread
- Needle

FOLDING INSTRUCTIONS
Lily Flowers: Flower A
Pages 103–104

1   If the paper is not already square, cut it into squares.

2   Fold a lily out of the square pieces of paper, following the instructions on pages 103–104. Pierce the base of the flower with a needle and thread the crochet thread through this hole so that you can hang the flower. Tie a knot in the thread below the flower to hold it in place. On the other end of the thread, thread on a small black bead, a faceted bead, and another small bead.

3   The flower can be hung from a branch or in a window. It also makes a lovely handmade gift.

Tip

There are many different kinds of transparent papers, both solid and patterned, available in craft supply stores. Let yourself be inspired.

Christmas Trees

in silver and white

FLOWER SIZE
approximately 2, 3, and 4 in. tall

MATERIALS
FOR EACH HANGER
- 14 sheets of white paper with a star pattern, 6 in. square
- Scrap amount of cardboard
- White or clear bead, ¼ in. in diameter
- 20 in. silver lurex thread
- Hole punch

FOLDING INSTRUCTIONS
Festive Flowers: Christmas Roses, Variation 4 (on this page)

Page 111

TEMPLATE
Page 125

1 Attach the bead to one end of the lurex thread with a knot or by gluing the end of the thread in the bead.

2 You will fold three flowers, each with six petals, following the directions for the Christmas Rose, Variation 4 (see below). Press the folded flower petals flat before gluing them together so that they are pointed.

3 Start by making the petals for the bottom flower from a 6 in. square of paper. Glue the petals together, placing the thread through the center of the flower with the bead at the bottom.

4 Cut six 5 in. squares of paper and fold them into petals for the medium-sized flower. Glue the petals together around the thread, above the first flower.

5 For the smallest flower, cut paper 3 in. square. Fold the petals and assemble them around the thread above the middle flower.

6 Cut out the star from silver paper (template on page 125) and punch holes where indicated. Thread the thread through the holes as shown in the photo.

Christmas Rose, Variation 4

Follow the first 13 steps for the Christmas Rose on page 111.

14 Fold both of the side corners inwards along the dashed lines.

15 Apply glue on the area outlined in yellow and fold the left side to the right to form a petal.

16 To glue the petals together, apply glue on the area outlined in yellow.

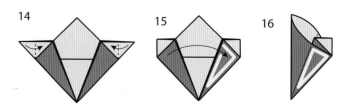

Materials and Tools

MINI CLOTHESPINS are used to hold pieces together while glue dries.

NYLON THREAD (0.2 mm in diameter) can be used as an unobtrusive hanger.

TWEEZERS are very helpful when handling the petals, flowers, and spheres.

If you want to cut your paper yourself, you'll need a CUTTER, METAL RULER, COMPASS, and CUTTING BOARD. You should always have SCISSORS on hand as well.

ALUMINUM WIRE (2 mm in diameter) can be used for stems. WIRE CUTTERS are needed to cut the wire.

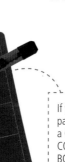

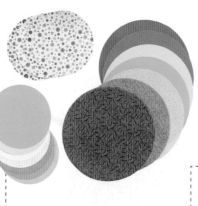

ALL-PURPOSE GLUE for paper is used to glue the flowers and flower petals. Solvent-free all-purpose glue is usually *not* suitable because it will cause the paper to curl.

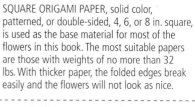

ROUND ORIGAMI PAPER, 4 and 6 in. in diameter, solid color or patterned, as well as DOILIES in different colors, 6 and 6½ in. in diameter, are used for the Anemone and Rose blossoms. Paper with a weight of 18 to 24 lbs. is the best choice for projects using round paper.

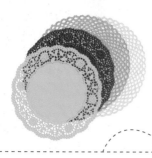

SQUARE ORIGAMI PAPER, solid color, patterned, or double-sided, 4, 6, or 8 in. square, is used as the base material for most of the flowers in this book. The most suitable papers are those with weights of no more than 32 lbs. With thicker paper, the folded edges break easily and the flowers will not look as nice.

Various ACCESSORIES, such as beads and rhinestones, are used for decoration.

PAPER BAKING CUPS, solid color, patterned, or two-sided, 2 in. in diameter on the bottom, can be substituted for round origami paper in many projects.

Difficulty Levels

Fast and simple

A little practice needed

Challenging

Folding Instructions

STAMEN FLOWERS

The first nine folding steps are the same for most variations of this flower (the one exception is the long petals for the floating flowers on pages 20–21).

1+2 Fold the paper square diagonally, crease the fold, then open it again. Apply glue on the spots indicated by the white line, and fold the bottom half up again.

3+4 Fold both of the corners to the middle on the dashed lines.

5, 6+7 Fold both the corners to the middle (to form a kite shape) and back out again.

8+9 Open the side in the direction of the arrow and press flat. The result is a kite shape.

10 Repeat steps 8 and 9 on the other side.

Continue with the instructions for the variation you would like fold.

Flowers with One Stamen

11+12 Fold the tips of the two kite shapes backwards along the dashed lines.

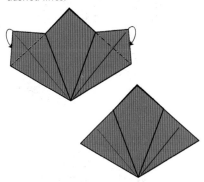

13 If the paper has a different colored front and back, fold the upper tip down. Skip this step if the paper is the same color on both sides.

14+15 Fold the triangle on the far right inward.

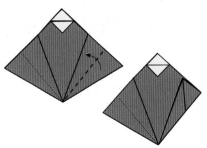

16 Repeat on the left side to form a square.

17+18 Apply glue to the part you folded inward on the right (outlined in white below) and bring it together with the corresponding part on the left to form a flower petal.

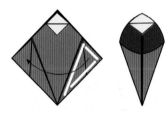

Flowers with Three Stamens

11+12 Fold the tip of the right kite shape down along the dashed line.

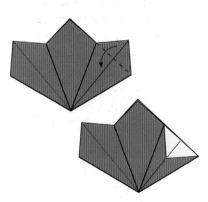

13+14 Fold the triangle on the far right inward.

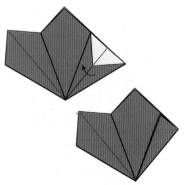

15 Repeat on the left side, forming a square.

16+17 If the paper has a different colored front and back, fold the upper tip down. Skip this step if the paper is the same color on both sides.

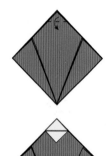

18+19 Apply glue to the part you folded inward on the right (outlined in white below) and bring it together with the corresponding part on the left to form a flower petal.

Flowers with a Ring of Stamens

11, 12+13 Fold the right half of the kite shape on the right inward along the dashed line. A small triangle the color of the back of the paper (if you are using paper with a different color on the back) will appear on the upper right. This is the color the stamens will be.

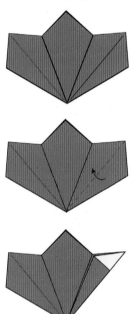

14 Fold this yellow triangle in half to the left and open it back up again.

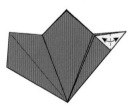

15 Fold the tip of the yellow triangle to the inside. If the back of the paper is a different color from the front, then you can fold the upper tip down along the dashed line.

16 Repeat steps 11 to 15 on the left side.

17+18 Apply glue to the folded section on the right (outlined in white below) and bring it together with the corresponding part on the left to form a flower petal. The stamens can be fanned out inside the petal to create the stamen ring.

Putting the Stamen Flowers Together

1 Each flower petal has a rounded side that faces outward, as well as two flat, triangular sides of the same size, to which the glue will be applied. Glue two flat sides of two petals together. You can use tweezers to press the petals together where you can't get to them with your fingers. Secure the petals with clothespins until the glue dries.

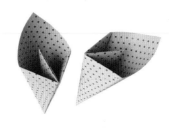

2 Here are the three flower petals glued together.

3 After gluing on the fourth petal, let the glue dry so that the flower petals do not shift when the fifth petal is added. This is what the finished flower looks like.

Putting the Stamen Flower Sphere Together

1 For a flower sphere you will need twelve flowers, each with five petals.

2 Hold two flowers together so that the petals touch in two places. Spread glue on the points of contact between the two flowers and attach them together. Secure them with two clothespins.

3 Add the third flower so that there are four points of contact between it and the first two flowers. Glue the flower in place at these four points and secure the flowers with clothespins.

4 Attach the fourth flower in the same way between any two flowers.

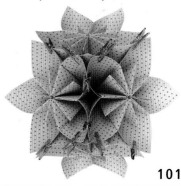

5 Add two more flowers. There are now six flowers and the half sphere is finished.

Tip
- - - - - - - - - - - - - - - - - -
From the fourth flower on, the flowers may not seem to fit in the spaces for them. Hold the blossoms in place with the help of the clothespins.

6 This is what the half sphere looks like on the bottom. You can now attach the thread for hanging the sphere; glue it across the middle of the half-sphere. Make sure that the thread runs between two flower petals on one side and across the middle of a flower petal on the other side. If you want, you can add a second thread to extend out the bottom of the sphere; when the the sphere is completely assembled and the glue is dry, you can attach beads or tassels to this thread. For this purpose, the thread needs to be at least 30 in. long.

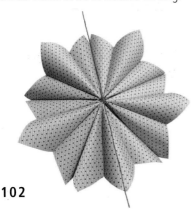

7 You will need to clamp the remaining six flowers in place with the clothespins as you glue them on. Use two clothespins on each petal for both of the last two flowers. In the picture below, the last flower is missing. The visible flower petals are not rounded anymore but almost flat. The green clothespins hold the last flower to be added.

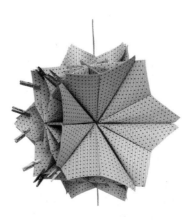

8 Put the final flower in place. Here you can clearly see how much this flower will need to be clamped to fit in this space.

9 Apply glue to one of the petals and secure it in place with clothespins. Next glue an opposite petal in place and secure with clothespins. Then attach the rest of the flower petals.

10 When the glue is completely dry you can remove all the clothespins.

LILY FLOWERS

Individual Lily Flowers

1+2 Fold the sheet in half and open it again; repeat on the other diagonal. Turn the sheet over.

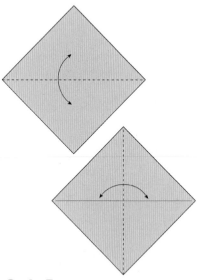

3, 4+5 Fold the sheet in half vertically and open it again; then fold it in half horizontally and open it again. Turn the sheet over.

6 The dashed diagonal lines are valley folds, and the dashed-and-dotted lines are mountain folds. Use these folds to collapse the sheet of paper into a smaller square (with the top open and the corner where all the sides come together at the bottom).

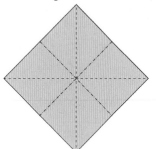

7 Open the triangular section on the right so it stands perpendicular to the rest of the piece. (Flower D is now finished; for the other variations, continue folding.)

8+9 Open up this section, then flatten it out to form a kite shape.

10 Open up and then flatten the other three sections in the same way. The whole piece should now be a kite shape.

11+12 Fold both of the upper corners of the top layer to the center along the dashed lines.

13 Repeat steps 11 and 12 three times, so the whole thing has a diamond shape.

14+15 Now open the top two folded corners and pull the layer underneath out and down, flattening it out to form a fold over the dashed line.

16+17 Fold the resulting downward-pointing triangle up along on the dashed line. Repeat the steps 14 to 17 on the other three sides. (Flower B is now finished; for Flowers A and C, go on.)

18 Open up the sides of the diamond so that the piece has a vertical fold line down the center on both sides.

19+20 Fold both of the lower edges in to the center.

103

21 Repeat on the other three sides. (Flower C is now finished. For Flower A, continue.)

22+23 Fold the tip down along the dashed line to form a petal.

24 Repeat on the other three sides.

25 Fold the flower petals up to about 90 degrees so that they stick out sideways.

Simple Lily Spheres

The sphere requires twenty individual lily flowers (Flower A) and four extra pieces of paper.

1 Roll up the flower petals of the lily flowers around a pencil or paint-brush handle to give them a rounded shape.

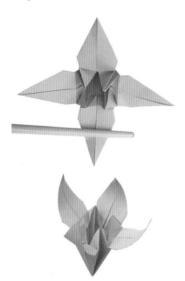

2a Cut out four paper circles. For flowers made with 4-inch square paper, cut circles 1 in. in diameter; for flowers made from 6-inch squares, cut circles 1¾ in. in diameter; and for flowers made from 8-inch squares, cut circles 3 in. in diameter.

2b With each circle, fold it down the center, then open it and fold it again, perpendicular to the first fold, so that the circle is in quarters. Turn the paper over and fold it in the same way twice more, so that the circle has eight sections.

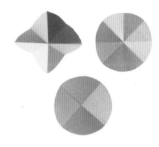

3+4 Glue the end of a lily flower into one of the creases in the circle. Repeat on the opposite side.

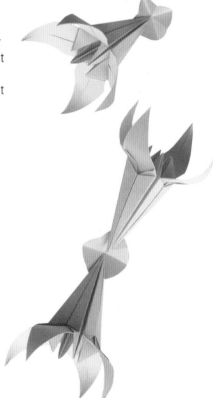

5 Glue on two more flowers.

6+7 Push the flowers together until the tips of the flower petals touch, and clamp them together with five small clothespins. This forms a quarter sphere.

8+9 Make another quarter sphere. Lay both quarter spheres on each other so that they form a half sphere. Hold the flower petals together with three clothespins.

10 This is what the half sphere looks like from the back. Glue both of the groups of four together in the middle, where the paper circles touch.

11 Create two more groups of four and put them together to form a half sphere in the same way. If you would like to hang this creation, attach the thread to the third or fourth group of four, using a needle to thread it through the circular piece.

12 Clip both half spheres together and glue the centers. When the glue is dry, remove the clothespins. Glue the four remaining flowers in the gaps visible between the groups. If you like, you can add more flowers afterward.

Lily Star Spheres

You need fourteen of Flower B (light blue here) and fourteen of Flower A (dark blue here).

1 Open up each Flower B as shown here.

2 For the middle star you need six Flower Bs.

3 Glue two of these flowers together at the base as shown.

4 Glue all six flowers together the same way.

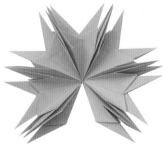

5 Stretch the entire thing a bit to bring the first flower around to meet the sixth one; glue them together.

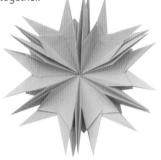

6 Roll the dark blue flower petals around a pencil or paintbrush handle to round the petals. Glue a dark blue flower inside each light-blue flower in the ring.

7 Glue on the hanging thread. On the right half of the light-blue star it should lie on top of a flower, on the left half it should be pulled in between two light-blue flowers.

8 Now glue four dark-blue flowers into four separate light-blue flowers.

9 Glue one of these double flowers on the ring as shown.

10 Glue three more double flowers on this side of the ring. Turn the piece over and glue on four more double flowers.

CALYX FLOWERS

Flower A

1 Fold the paper square on the diagonal and then open it.

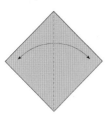

2+3 Fold the right corner to the middle fold line.

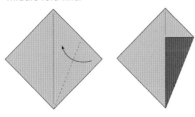

4+5 Fold the right corner to the center again, along the dashed line.

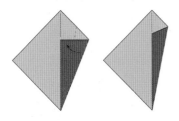

6 Repeat steps 2 to 5 on the left. The piece will have a kite shape.

7 Unfold the kite shape completely. Fold the outermost section on the right inward.

8+9 Fold the leftmost section inward. Apply glue on the right folded section (outlined in white below left) and then fold the left half to the right. Open the resulting flower petal at the top like a bag. Glue together five of these flower petals to form a flower, applying glue to the section outlined in white in the picture below right. When the fifth petal is glued to the fourth, allow the glue to dry completely. Then you can glue the first and last petals together.

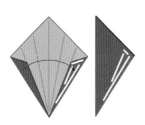

Tip: You could also make a flower with more or fewer petals.

Flower B

1,2+3 Make an angle template from cardboard (see template on page 125; the size to use will be indicated in the project instructions). Place the template (shown in green) at the top of the paper and then fold the bottom edge up to the edge of the template.

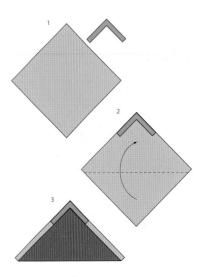

4 Remove the template and fold the piece in half, then open it up again.

5+6 Fold the right corner up to the top of the piece along the dotted line. Repeat on the left.

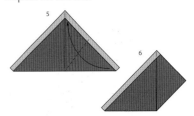

7 + 8 Fold the right corner along the dotted line to meet the center line.

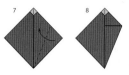

9 + 10 Repeat on the left side. Open the last fold on each side to form a square.

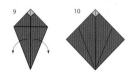

11, 12 + 13 Open the upper triangle on the right side and flatten it out. Repeat on the left side.

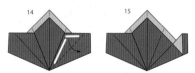

14 + 15 Apply glue where marked with white lines below and fold this flap down.

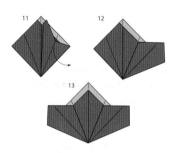

16 + 17 Repeat steps 14 and 15 on the left side. Apply glue to the bottom part of the folded section on the right (outlined in white in illustration 16) and bring the corresponding part on the left over to meet it. Make three or four more flower petals in the same way. Then apply glue over the bottom part of the glued section (outlined in white in illustration 17) and glue the flower petals together to form a flower. Let the glue dry completely after gluing the last

petal on; once the glue is dry, glue the first and last petals together.

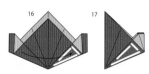

Tip: When folding this flower, you can either fold the sides one at a time or do each step on both sides before moving on to the next step.

Flower C

1, 2 + 3 Make an angle template from cardboard (see template on page 125; the size to use will be indicated in the project instructions). Place the template (shown in green) at the top of the paper and then fold the bottom edge up to the edge of the template. Apply glue on the bottom half of the paper (white lines) to hold the papers together during folding.

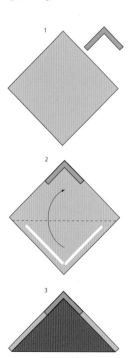

4 Fold the right half gently to the left and then back without creasing the fold. This will result in a rounded, not pointed, petal (for a more angular flower, you can crease the fold).

5 Fold the right corner up to the top along the dashed line and then fold it back.

6 + 7 Fold up the right corner up to the fold line just made.

8 + 9 Repeat steps 5–7 on the left side. Apply glue on the right folded section (marked with white lines) and fold the left side to the right. Apply glue to the finished flower petal where marked below and attach the next petal to it. When you have five petals glued together, let the glue dry completely before gluing the first and last petals together.

Six-Flower Spheres

A six-flower sphere is structured like a cube, with each of the six sides being replaced with a flower.

1+2 Fold and assemble six individual flowers (Calyx Flower B or C), each made with with four petals.

4 Glue the third flower onto the first and second flowers, with its petals touching each original flower's petals in two places, as before, and secure it with mini clothespins. Half of the sphere is now finished.

6 To complete the sphere, attach the fourth flower.

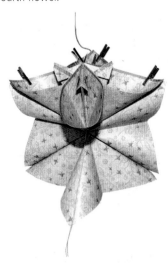

5 This is what the half sphere looks like on the bottom. If you would like to hang this sphere, add a hanging thread and secure with plenty of glue. You can leave a length of thread hanging out the bottom, if desired, to thread beads onto.

7 Add the last two flowers in the same way, and the six-flowered sphere is now finished.

3 Put two flowers together so that two pairs of petals touch. Apply glue at these locations and then hold the flowers together with mini clothespins.

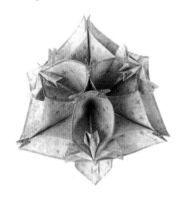

Half-Spheres and Twelve-Flower Spheres

1 You will need six individual flowers for the half-sphere and twelve for the full sphere. Use Calyx Flower B or C, with five petals in each flower.

2 Glue two flowers together at the points of the petals, holding them together with mini clothespins.

3 Add a third flower in the same way. Due to the angle of the flower petal tips, you will need to twist the petals a little. This will always be the case when you glue three flower petal tips together; don't let it bother you.

4 Glue on the fourth flower and secure it with mini clothespins (shown here attached with green clothespins).

5 Add the fifth flower right next to the fourth flower (blue clothespins).

6 Add the sixth flower right next to the fifth flower (red clothespins). The half sphere is now finished.

7 This is what the half sphere looks like on the bottom. Our middle flower has a small red wooden bead (¼ in. in diameter) for hanging the twelve-flower sphere. To hang this sphere: Before you assemble the flowers, tie a knot at the end of a length of hanging thread and thread a bead onto it. Lay the hanging thread through the middle of a flower when you are gluing it together, with the bead at the bottom of the flower. This flower will be the top of the hanging sphere.

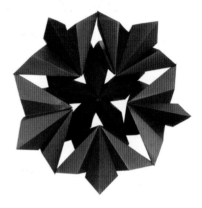

8 Create a second half-sphere from six more flowers. Glue both half spheres together to form a full twelve-flower sphere.

FESTIVE FLOWERS

Christmas Roses

1+2 Fold the paper square diagonally.

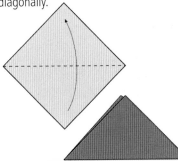

3 Fold both of the corners to the middle along the dashed lines, then open them back up.

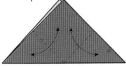

4+5 Fold the front tip down along the dashed line.

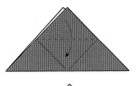

6+7 Fold the two corners to the middle again, the same way you did in step 3, to form a square.

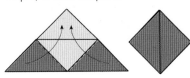

8 Fold both sides in to the middle to create a kite shape.

9+10 Unfold the kite shape completely on both sides to return to a large triangle.

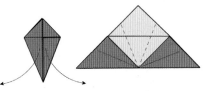

11+12 Hold down the paper above the dotted-and-dashed line and pull up the portion of the corner below that line. Open it up and fold it up to the top fold line (the dashed line in the illustration below), flattening it out into a kite shape. Repeat on the other side.

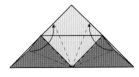

13 Fold the outer half of each kite inward.

14 Apply glue to the right side of the piece on the small triangle (outlined in yellow) and fold the left half over to the right.

15 To glue the petals together, apply glue to the area outlined in yellow and add the next petal. Continue until you have the full number of petals required for your project.

Winter Aconites

Tip: The first twelve folding steps are identical to the first twelve steps of the Christmas Rose.

13+14 Fold the upper half of each kite shape down.

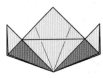

15+16 Fold the corner of the upper layer only inward along the dashed lines on each side.

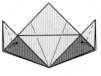

17+18 Fold the entire side triangle inward on each side.

19 Fold both of the upper corners down along the dashed lines.

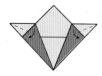

20 Apply glue on the area outlined in yellow and fold the left side to the right to form a petal.

21 To glue the petals together, apply glue to the area outlined in yellow below and attach another petal. Continue until the required number of petals is reached.

Festive Flower Spheres

These flower spheres are always made of twelve individual flowers, with each flower having five petals. They are assembled the same way as the stamen flower spheres (see pages 101–102).

1 The individual flower consists of five flower petals (Winter Aconite flowers are shown here).

2 Hold two individual flowers together so that two pairs of petals are touching. Apply glue on these areas and then hold the flowers together with two clothespins.

3 Lay on the third individual flower, apply glue where the petals touch, and secure the flower with a clothespin.

4, 5, 6 Next, glue on flowers four, five, and six. Half of the flower sphere is now finished.

7 This is what the half sphere looks like on the bottom. At this point, attach the hanging thread, using plenty of glue to secure it.

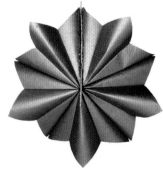

8 Continue adding flowers until you have eleven flowers in the sphere.

9+10 When you add the twelfth flower, there will be plenty of space around it. Stretch out the flower to reach the corresponding petals and pin it in place while the glue dries. Start by gluing two pairs of petals on opposite sides of the flower.

11 Next, attach another petal on the left side (where there are still two free flower petals), then the petal opposite it. Lastly, glue on the remaining flower petal on the left side.

12 This is what the finished flower sphere looks like.

13 Here is what the flower sphere looks like with leaves added.

ANEMONE FLOWERS

Flower A

1 Fold the paper circle in half and open it up again.

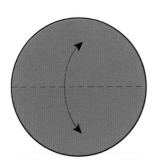

2 Turn the paper 90 degrees, fold it in half, and open it up again. You should see two fold lines that cross in the middle of the circle. Now turn the paper over.

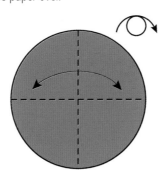

3 The fold lines are now mountain folds (dashed-and-dotted lines). Take one of these fold lines (a) and bring it up to meet the next one (b); crease the center to form a valley fold (c; dashed line). Open the fold again.

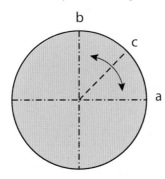

4 Repeat this process with the original mountain fold (a) and the one on the opposite side (d) to form another valley fold (d).

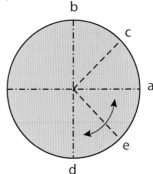

5 Turn the paper over again. Now the mountain folds are valley folds and vice versa.

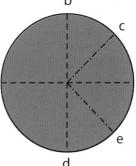

6 Fold the lower half of the circle up and fold the right side of the piece in to the center, using the mountain and valley folds you just created.

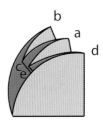

7 Apply a line of glue on the edges of the inner folds (marked with yellow below) and press them together. The flower petal is finished.

8 Once you have made the required number of petals, glue them together, applying glue just on the inner edge of each petal (yellow line). Be very precise when fitting the petals together, as they must fit exactly for a neat, beautiful final flower. Once you have all the petals glued together, glue the last petal to the first one to form the blossom.

1 Fold the paper circle in half from side to side and open it up again, forming a vertical valley fold (dashed line). Then turn the paper over.

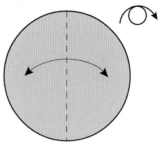

2 The vertical fold is now a mountain fold (dashed-and-dotted line). Fold the paper in half from top to bottom and open it up again (forming a horizontal valley fold).

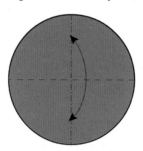

3 Fold the right side of the valley fold (a) to the top of the mountain fold (b) and crease the center to form another valley fold (c). Open the piece up again.

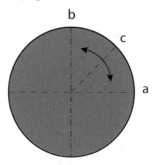

4 Do the same on the bottom half of the circle (folds a and d).

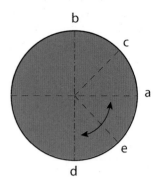

5 Before folding up the lower half of the circle, apply glue to the left of the vertical mountain fold (yellow line).

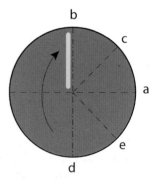

6 Fold up the lower half of the circle so that folds line up with b and d together, as well as c and e.

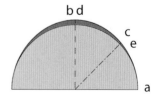

Flower C

7 Apply a line of glue just to the right of fold line d (yellow line). Open up the right side of the piece and flatten it out perpendicular to the piece, bringing fold line e to the left. Press the piece so the glue adheres.

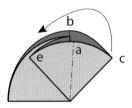

8 Glue and fold the back of the piece in the same way, bringing fold line c to the left.

9 Fold the required number of petals. Apply a vertical line of glue to the edge of the first flower petal (yellow line), lay another flower petal on top of it, and press. Add the rest of the petals in the same way, then glue the last flower petal to the first.

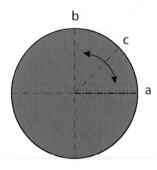

1 Fold the paper circle in half.

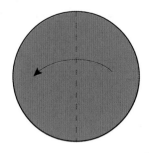

2 Fold the resulting semicircle in half.

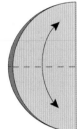

3 Open up all of the folds. You should have a continuous vertical valley fold (dashed line) with a horizontal valley fold on the left side and a horizontal mountain fold (dashed-and-dotted line) on the right side.

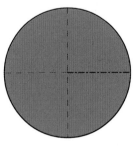

4 Bring the mountain fold (a) up to meet the top of the vertical fold (b); crease the edge to form valley fold c. Open the piece up again.

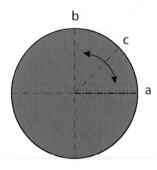

5 Repeat step 4 on the lower half with folds a and d to form fold e.

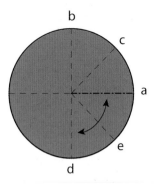

6 Fold the lower half of the semicircle up, and at the same time bring fold a inward, folding the piece along the fold lines you just made. Glue the two right edges together on the inside (marked with a yellow line). The flower petal is finished.

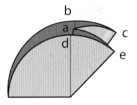

7 Fold and glue the required number of petals. When you are ready to assemble them into a flower, apply glue to the area outlined in yellow and press the petals together. Once all the petals are glued together, glue the last petal to the first one.

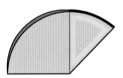

ROSE FLOWERS

Working with Doilies

Since doilies are made from very thin paper, they can sometimes stick together. Make sure you are working with only a single layer of paper. It's a good idea to check again just before you glue the petals, since at this point it is still easy to correct the problem if you did end up with two sheets.

If the doilies have protruding parts on the edges, you may want to trim them off while the papers are still all together. Otherwise, you might have to trim each sheet individually.

Finding the Center of the Paper

For the flower petals to fit together well, you must fold each one the same way. Doilies are symmetrical, but there is some variation within the lacy edge. Some have a fold line that suits them best; this line is often marked by an embossed print on the inside.

If the suggested fold line is missing, you should pick one. For instance, for a doily with six roses around the edge, you might orient it with a rose at the center at the top and bottom, then create your center fold line by bringing the two roses together, lining them up exactly with each other. The scallops on the edges should match—if not, try a different folding orientation. Once you have picked a fold line, use the same line for all the petals.

Remember that doily paper is very delicate. You can crease the solid center of the doily with a fingernail or bone folder, but on the lacy outer part you should just press gently to avoid tearing the paper.

Gluing Doilies Together

When gluing doilies together it is inevitable that glue will run through the lacy edge. Therefore it is important to use only a small amount glue. Open the flower petal with tweezers immediately after gluing and pinning it to keep the areas that should not be glued from sticking together. Wipe up excess glue with your fingertips (wash your hands beforehand), then rub your fingertips together to dry the glue so you can remove it from your hands. Excess glue deep inside the petal can be removed with tweezers.

Work very carefully with the colored lace paper—here the glue is noticeably more visible than on white paper.

Let the finished flower petal dry. As when gluing the petal together, if you combine the petals to form a flower or combine flowers to form a sphere, you must immediately wipe up any excess glue with your fingertips.

Working with Paper Baking Cups

When working with baking cups with pleated edges, you do not need to be as precise as when folding a round sheet of paper. Slight unevenness doesn't destroy the overall effect of the flower because, with the pleats, all of the folded areas still look the same.

Start by pressing the baking cup flat and folding it in half to get a semicircle. Then proceed to fold it just like an ordinary sheet of origami paper.

Flower A

1 and 2 Fold the paper in half. Fold the resulting semicircle in half again, then open it up.

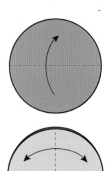

3 Fold the upper layer down along the red dashed line.

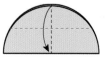

4 Fold both sides to the center and back out again.

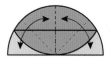

5 and 6 Next fold both of the sides up to the fold line just created.

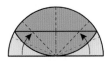

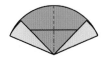

7 Apply glue to the right folded portion (outlined in yellow) and bring the left half to meet it. The flower petal is finished.

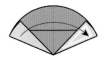

8 When you have enough petals for a flower, apply glue to the section outlined in yellow below and glue the petals together.

Variation 1

Steps 1 to 6 are identical to the regular instructions for Flower A.

7 and 8 Fold down the upper corner of each folded section along the red dashed line. Open up the fold, apply glue to the top portion (outlined in yellow), and fold it down again.

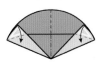

9 Apply glue to the right folded portion (outlined in yellow) and bring the left half over to meet it. The flower petal is now finished.

10 Glue the completed flower petals together by applying glue on the portion indicated below.

Variation 2

Steps 1 to 6 are identical to the regular instructions for Flower A.

7 and 8 Fold in the outer corner of each folded section along the red dashed line. Open up the fold, apply glue to the outermost portion (outlined in yellow), and fold it in again.

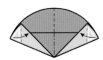

9 Apply glue to the right folded portion (outlined in yellow), except for the part that you just folded inward, and bring the left half over to meet it. The flower petal is now finished.

10 Glue the completed flower petals together by applying glue on the portion indicated here.

Flower B

1 Fold the paper in half. Fold the resulting semicircle in half again, then open it up.

2 and 3 Fold the upper half down along the red dashed line.

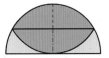

4 and 5 Now fold both sides up to the middle.

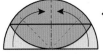

6 Fold both sides to the middle again and unfold.

7 and 8 Open all the side folds to return to a semicircle shape.

9 and 10 Fold both of the lower sections up along the red lines.

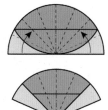

11, 12 and 13 Lift the middle section on the red line in the direction of the arrow so that this section can be folded forward. Apply glue on the folded part on the right (outlined in yellow), and bring the left half over to meet to the right. Make the other flower petals the same way.

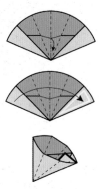

14 Glue each flower petal to the next by applying glue to the section outlined in yellow.

Variation 1

Steps 1 to 10 are identical to the regular instructions for Flower B.

11 and 12 Fold down the upper corner of each of the sections you just folded inward, along the red line.

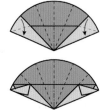

13, 14 and 15 Lift the middle section on the red line in the direction of the arrow so that this section can be folded forward. Apply glue on the folded part on the right (outlined in yellow), and bring the left half over to meet to the right. Make the other flower petals the same way.

16 Glue each flower petal to the next by applying glue to the section outlined in yellow.

Variation 2

Steps 1 to 10 are identical to the regular instructions for Flower B.

11 and 12 Fold up each side again, along the red dashed lines.

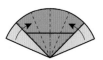

13 Apply glue on the folded part on the right (outlined in yellow), and bring the left half over to meet to the right. Make the other flower petals the same way.

16 Glue each flower petal to the next by applying glue to the section outlined in yellow.

Rose Flower Spheres

Tip: These flower spheres are composed of six flowers with four petals each. You will need twenty-four folded and glued flower petals (Flower B, regular instructions or Variation 1).

1 Glue the flower petals together in fours to form six flowers.

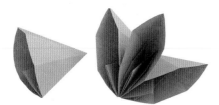

2 This is what the finished flower looks like.

3 Insert a hanging thread in the middle of the sixth flower. Set this flower aside, as it will be added last.

4 Put two flowers together so that their petals touch in two places. Spread glue on these areas, then stick the flowers together, securing them with mini clothespins (red here).

5 Add the third flower. This time there are four areas where the petals are touching; all should be glued. Secure the flower again with clothespins (yellow here).

6 This is what the half sphere looks like on the bottom.

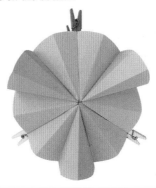

7 Glue on the fourth flower and secure it with mini clothespins (white here).

8 Add on the fifth flower and secure it with mini clothespins (green here).

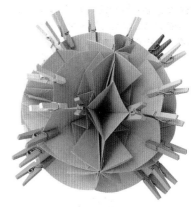

9 Turn the entire sphere over. There is a flat area where the sixth flower will be glued on—it is clearly larger than the flower.

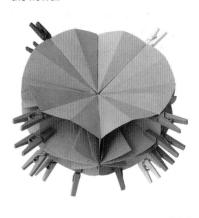

119

10 Add the flower with the hanging thread glued through the middle. Begin by gluing on only one of its petals; secure it with two clothespins (dark-blue here).

11 Now glue on the opposite flower petal of the sixth flower and secure it with two mini clothespins. You will have to stretch it quite a bit. Tweezers can be very helpful when you are putting the flowers together. Due to the tension, all six flowers are stretched a bit, and the central opening in each flower will get a little bigger.

12 Next, glue on the third flower petal and secure it with mini clothespins (red here).

13 Now glue on the fourth and last flower petal and secure it with mini clothespins (yellow here). The sphere is now finished.

14 When the glue is completely dry, you can remove the clothespins.

Tip: The last flower will have to stretch a lot (as will the other flowers when the last one is added). It is important to let the glue on the rest of the sphere dry before adding the last flower so that the whole sphere can take up the tension without being pulled apart.

GARDEN FLOWERS

Paper for Outdoor Use

You can find weatherproof paper in many designs: white, colored on one side, or patterned. This paper is heavier, and therefore more difficult to fold, than regular paper. While the paper is water-resistant, it will eventually wear away.

If your paper is not already cut to size, you can cut any suitable paper with the help of a paper-cutting machine or a cutter and steel ruler on a cutting board.

Simple Flowers

1 Fold the square of paper in half diagonally.

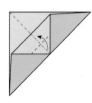

2 Fold the resulting triangle in half and open it again.

3+4 Fold down the tip of the upper layer along the red line.

5 Fold up the same tip along the red line.

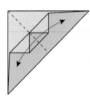

6 Fold the whole piece in half along the red line and open it up again.

7+8 Fold both of the corners to the center to form a square.

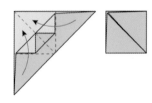

9 Fold the corners of the square to the center so that a kite shape is created.

10+11 Open the kite shape up into a triangle again.

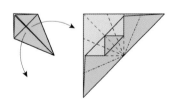

12 Continue to open the triangle to get the shape shown below, then apply glue on both of the places marked with yellow lines and fold the piece back into a triangle.

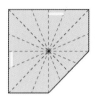

13+14 Fold the outer corners up along the red lines.

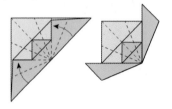

15 Apply glue on one of the folded portions (outlined in yellow) and fold the opposite one to meet it to form a flower petal.

16 Once you have made all the petals needed for your project, glue them together by applying glue to the area outlined in yellow below.

Two-Part Flower

Outer Petals

1+2   Use a ¼ in. angle template (see the templates on page 125) to leave a margin of ¼ in. around the edge when you make the first diagonal fold.

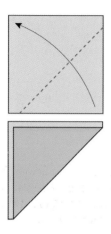

3   Fold the triangle in half, then open it again.

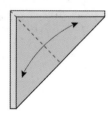

4+5   Fold both of the corners to the center to form a square.

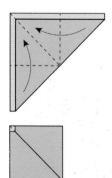

6   Fold the corners of the square to the center to create a kite shape.

7+8   Open up the kite shape to return to the triangle shape.

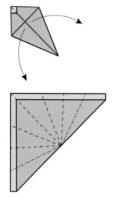

9+10   Fold the outermost triangles in along the red lines.

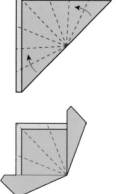

11   Apply glue to one of the areas you just folded inward (outlined in yellow) and fold the left half over to the right to form a flower petal.

12   Once all the petals are folded and glued, attach them together by applying glue on the area outlined in yellow below.

Inner Petals

For this variation, skip folding step 3 and proceed with steps 4 through 10 as normal.

11a   Before gluing the left half to the right half, fold the tips of the side pieces backward along the red lines.

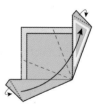

12a   The finished flower petal does not have a fold line because step 3 was left out. Glue the flower petals together in fours to form flowers by applying glue on the area outlined in yellow.

Garden Flower Spheres

1+2 For this sphere, you need six flowers, each with four flower petals.

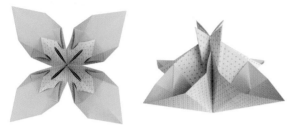

3 Glue a hanging thread through the middle of one of the flowers as you assemble it.

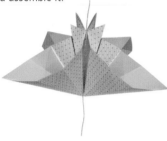

4 When you glue the flowers together, apply streaks of glue to only the edges of the petals.

5 Glue two flowers together and secure with clothespins until the glue is dry.

6 Glue on a third flower the same way. Secure the glued areas with six clothespins (dark here). Half of the sphere is finished.

7 Create a second half-sphere from three flowers. Remove the clothespins after the glue is dry. Place the two spheres together back to back; glue the edges of the petals together and secure with clothespins until dry.

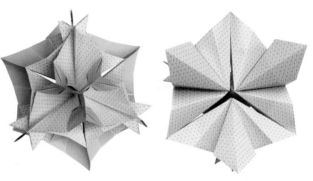

8 This is what the finished sphere looks like.

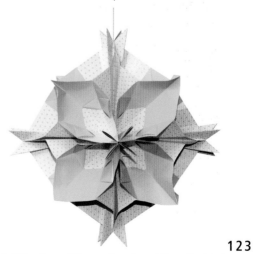

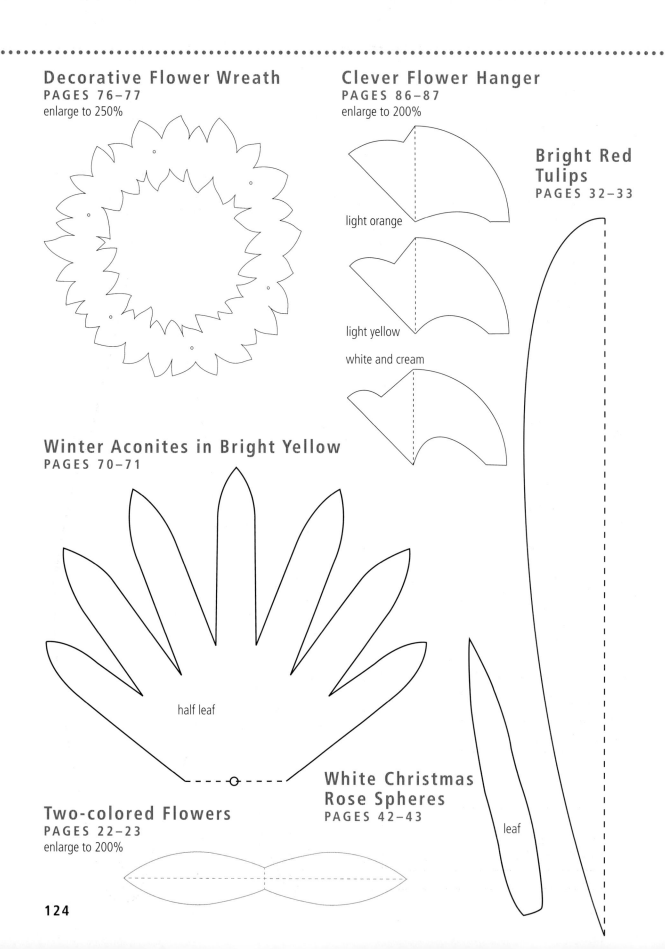

Decorative Flower Wreath
PAGES 76–77
enlarge to 250%

Clever Flower Hanger
PAGES 86–87
enlarge to 200%

light orange

light yellow

white and cream

Bright Red Tulips
PAGES 32–33

Winter Aconites in Bright Yellow
PAGES 70–71

half leaf

White Christmas Rose Spheres
PAGES 42–43

Two-colored Flowers
PAGES 22–23
enlarge to 200%

leaf

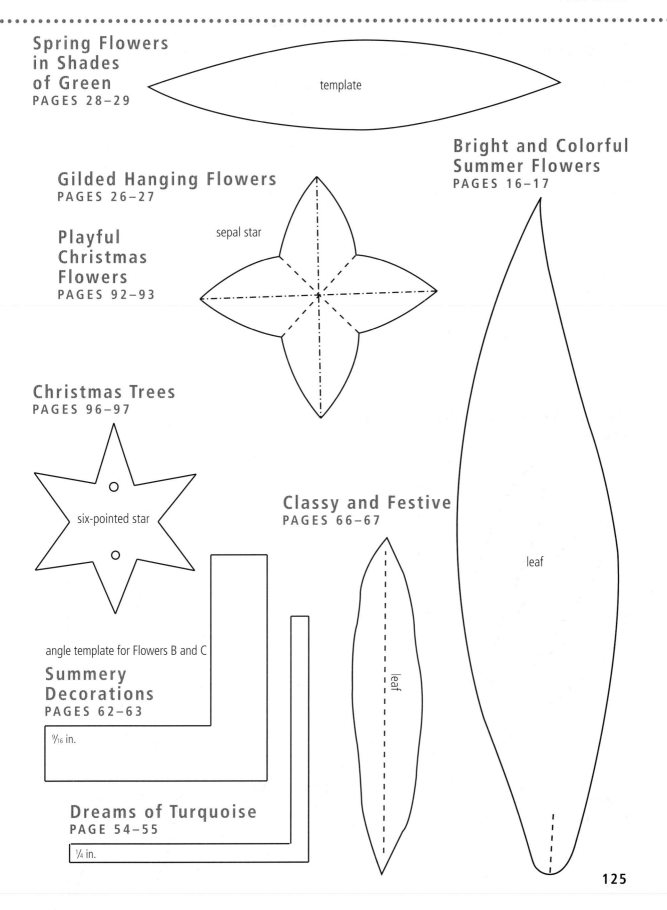

Spring Flowers in Shades of Green
PAGES 28–29

template

Bright and Colorful Summer Flowers
PAGES 16–17

Gilded Hanging Flowers
PAGES 26–27

Playful Christmas Flowers
PAGES 92–93

sepal star

Christmas Trees
PAGES 96–97

six-pointed star

Classy and Festive
PAGES 66–67

leaf

angle template for Flowers B and C

Summery Decorations
PAGES 62–63

$^9/_{16}$ in.

leaf

Dreams of Turquoise
PAGE 54–55

$^1/_4$ in.

Photos: frechverlag GmbH, 70499 Stuttgart; Light Point, Michael Ruder, Stuttgart,
    Armin Taeubner (all working photos and cuts)
Drawings: Armin Taeubner
Production Management and Editing: Alice Hoernecke, Claudia Mack
Layout: Sophie Hoepfner
Print and Binding: Graspo CZ, Czech Republic
Translation: Dustin Noll
Cover design: Wendy Reynolds

The original German edition of this book was published as *Fleurogami für alle.*
Copyright © 2013 by frechverlag GmbH, Stuttgart, Germany (www.frech.de)
This edition is published by arrangement with Claudia Böhme Rights & Literary Agency,
    Hannover, Germany (www.agency-boehme.com).
Copyright © 2014 by Stackpole Books

Published by
STACKPOLE BOOKS
5067 Ritter Road
Mechanicsburg, PA 17055
www.stackpolebooks.com

All rights reserved, including the right to reproduce this book or portions thereof in any
form or by any means, electronic or mechanical, including photocopying, recording, or by
any information storage and retrieval system, without permission in writing from the
publisher. All inquiries should be addressed to Stackpole Books, 5067 Ritter Road,
Mechanicsburg, PA 17055.

Printed in U.S.A.
10 9 8 7 6 5 4 3 2 1
First edition

Library of Congress Cataloging-in-Publication Data

Tdubner, Armin.
   [Fleurogami fur alle. English]
   Floragami / Armin Tdubner.
        pages cm
   Translation of: Fleurogami fur alle.
   ISBN 978-0-8117-1336-8
   1. Paper flowers.   2. Origami.   I. Title.
   TT892.T3813 2014
   736'.982—dc23
                    2013041546